Dutch for Beginners

*A Comprehensive Guide for Learning
the Dutch Language Fast*

NOTE: The vocabularies of this book are spread over the content. Each vocabulary is with the conversation or topic it belongs to. This prevents having a long list at the end of the book. Moreover, the learning of new words will be more gradual, and therefore, more pleasant. You might find some overlap, but that is just part of the learning process.

Contents

Introduction

So, you want to learn Dutch—and fast! Well, although the learning process will be fun, be prepared, too, because Dutch grammar and spelling are mostly illogical. Do not despair, though; you will learn to shrug and move on. Plus, the Dutch admire people who try to speak their language, and they want to practice their English with you. They pride themselves on speaking several languages, which is a necessity since relatively few people speak Dutch. Straightforwardness is also part of their culture, so be sure to take the lead in a conversation. Be bold, but in a pleasant way!

In this book, you will not only discover the basics of the Dutch language but also learn more about the Dutch people, such as their habits and behaviors. Make sure to be open-minded with the correction of your pronunciation, words, and conjugations. Ask your family, friends, or fellow students to test you as you go.

Before long, you will have mastered *Dutch for Beginners*!

Part 1 – The Very Basics

The Dutch Alphabet

The Dutch alphabet is like the English alphabet, but with different names to spell each letter, like when you have to do that on the phone, e.g.:

A – Anna, Anton

B – Bernard

C – Cornelis

D – Dirk

E – Eduard

F – Ferdinand

G – Gerard

H – Hendrik

I – Isaak, Izaak

J – Jan, Johannes

K – Karel

L – Lodewijk

M - Maria, Marie

N - Nico

O - Otto

P - Pieter

Q - Quotiënt, Quirinus

R - Rudolf

S - Simon

T - Teunis, Theodoor, Tinus

U - Utrecht

V - Victor

W - Willem

X - Xantippe

Y - Ypsilon

IJ - IJsbrand

Z - Zaandam, Zacharias

Some letters in Dutch are pronounced differently than they are in English:

A - English: "ay" Dutch: "aaa"

B - English: "beee" Dutch: "bay"

C - English: "see" Dutch: "say"

D - English: "dee" Dutch: "day"

E - English: "ee" Dutch: "ey"

F - the same

G: English: "gjeee" Dutch: "guh", with a throat sound (as if you have to cough or there's pressure on your windpipe)

H - English: "8tsh" Dutch: "haa"

I - English: "eye" Dutch: "ee"

J - English: "jay" Dutch: "yay"

K - English: "kay" Dutch: "kaaa"

L - the same

M - the same

N - the same

O - the same

P - English: "pee" Dutch: "pay"

Q - English: "cue" Dutch: "cu"

R - English: "are" Dutch: "eerrr"

S - the same

T - English: "tea" Dutch: "tay"

U - English: "you" Dutch: "uuu"

V - English: "vie" Dutch: "vay"

W - English: "double U" Dutch: say "wey" (although Dutch are known for "Double Dutch," they don't double in the alphabet)

X - English: "ex" Dutch: "ix"

Y - English: "why" Dutch: "i grèck"

IJ - English: - Dutch: "ei"

Z - the same

See? Not hard at all! Try to speak the letters of the alphabet out loud a few times, to get the hang of it. They should not be twisting your tongue—yet—so you can grow accustomed to them pretty fast.

Counting

Small children are very proud when they can count in their own language—and even prouder when they can throw in a few numbers in another language. It is time to make you proud as well:

> 1. een - "eyn"
>
> 2. twee - "twey"

3. drie – "drea"

4. vier – "vear"

5. vijf - "veif"

6. zes – "cès"

7. zeven – "zayven"

8. acht – "agggt"

9. negen – "naygggen"

10. tien – "tean"

Did you observe that 8 has a ch, a double consonant? CH is pronounced like the G, so cough and you will pronounce it correctly. There are some more of these doubles, but they are detailed later on.

Continue counting:

11. elf – "elv"

12. twaalf – "twaalf"

13. dertien – "dairteen"

14. veertien – "veerteen"

15. vijftien – "veifteen"

16. zestien – "cèsteen"

17. zeventien – "zayventeen"

18. achttien – "agggteen"

19. negentien – "naygggenteen"

20. twintig – "twintigggg"

Don't give up! From now on, it is as easy as pie...

21 - eenentwintig – "eynENtwintiggg" and so on...

22 – tweeëntwintig

23 – drieëntwintig

24 – vierentwintig

25 – vijfentwintig

26 – zesentwintig

27 – zevenentwintig

28 – achtentwintig

29 – negenentwintig

30 – dertig

It is easy to break down the way you count over 20. However, the Dutch do it the other way around, so different from what you are used to in English. So, 23 is like 3 and 20 = 3 en 20; 26 is 6 and 20 = 6 en 20. It goes on like that up to 100.

The tens:

10 – "teen"

20 – "twintiggg"

30 – "dèrtiggg"

40 – "faertigggg"

50 – "veiftiggg"

60 – "cèstiggg"

70 – "zayventiggg"

80 – "taggtig" (mind the t!)

90 – "naygggentigg"

100 – honderd = "hondurt"

101– honderdeen

102 – honderdtwee

130 – honderddertig

165 – honderdvijfenzestig

200 – tweehonderd

300 – driehonderd

1000 – "duycent"

Of course, once you see the logic of it, you can learn this by heart. Test yourself to see if you really know how to count:

Tiny task #1:

13 = 8 = ; 27 = ; 63 = ; 78 = ; 104 = ; 12 = ; 140 = ; 549 = ; 636 = ; 244 = ; 82 = . How to say it in Dutch? Check the answers at the end of the book!

The Days of the Week

Unlike in English, Dutch does not use a capital letter for the days of the week.

Monday – maandag "maandaggg"

Tuesday – dinsdag "dinzdaggg"

Wednesday – woensdag "wunzdaggg"

Thursday – donderdag "dondurdaggg"

Friday – vrijdag "vreidaggg"

Saturday – zaterdag "zaturdaggg"

Sunday – zondag "zòndaggg"

The day has a morning, afternoon, evening, and night.

Morning – ochtend or morgen "morgggen"

Afternoon – middag "middaggg"

Evening – avond "afont"

Night – nacht "nagggtt"

Dutch glues the two words together when they want to indicate a specific part of the day: Monday evening – maandagavond; Saturday afternoon – zaterdagmiddag.

The Months of the Year

January – januari "jànywari"

February – februari "fèbrywari"

March – maart "maaart"

April – april "àpril"

May – mei "meiii"

June – juni "juuniii"

July – juli "juuuliii"

August – augustus "ouwgustus"

September – september

October – oktober

November – november

December – december "deycember"

Did you spot a resemblance with the days of the week? Yes! No capitals used for the months, either! And... some of the months have the same pronunciation in both English and Dutch.

Dutch use dates a bit differently than English. Dutch gives the day first, then the month.

For instance: April 14 = 14 april; June 8 = 8 juni

You can take this a bit further: 2020, April 14 = 14 april 2020; 2020, June 8 = 8 juni 2020

Watches and Clocks

You need the time every moment of the day, so telling the time is very important. Trains, buses, planes, work, school—everything works with time and punctuality (hopefully). So, it is vital to know all about the time!

To start, the Dutch do not use a.m. and p.m. Timetables run on a 24-hour scheme, so a train may leave the station at 14:12 hours, 02:12 p.m. Dutch also don't say "14 hours"; they say, "the train leaves at 12 past two." Only when it is not clear if it's the afternoon or the middle of the night, do they say: the train leaves at 12 past two this afternoon (vanmiddag) or tonight (vannacht). Of course, now, with digital clocks taking over, Dutch keeps on counting till 24. 24:00 hours is also 00:00 hours. And although the digital watch or clock is telling you it is 14:15, Dutch people say, "het is kwart over twee" ("it is a quarter past two.") Confused? Don't be—you will get the hang of it!

Here are some digital examples:

10:05 – het is vijf over tien (it is five past ten)

10:15 – het is kwart over tien (it is a quarter past ten)

10:25 – het is vijf voor half 11 (it is 25 past ten)

10:30 – het is half 11 (it is half past ten)

10:40 – het is tien over half 11 (it is 20 to 11)

15:00 – het is drie uur (it is three o'clock p.m.)

15:10 – het is tien over drie (it is ten past three)

15:20 – het is tien voor half vier (it is 20 past three)

15:35 – het is vijf over half vier (it is 25 to four)

15:45 – het is kwart voor vier (it is a quarter to four)

Notice the Dutch use "over" for the first 15 minutes after the whole hour, then go to "voor" towards the half hour. The same goes for the first 15 minutes after the half hour and the last 15 minutes towards the whole hour. Once you notice how it works, it is simple!

Some practical lines:

Ik zie je om drie uur – I will see you at three

Hij is (te) laat – He is (too) late

Jullie zijn alwéér te laat – You are late again

Zij is altijd precies op tijd – She is always right on time

Weet jij/u hoe laat het is? - Do you have/Can you tell me the time?

Kom niet te laat! - Don't be late!

Colorful Life – Vocabulary of Colors

What would life be without any color? Boring, dull, depressing? Fortunately, there are a lot of colors to paint one's days and experiences with.

To start, here are the colors of the Dutch flag: red/white/blue.

rood - red

donkerrood - dark red

lichtrood - light red

wit - white

crème - off white

blauw - blue

donkerblauw - dark blue

lichtblauw - light blue*

*You get it, right? "donker" - dark and "licht" - light (in any color, except for black and white).

beige - beige/caramel

bruin - brown

geel - a

grijs - gray

groen - green

khaki - khaki

lila - violet

olijfgroen – olive green

oranje – orange

paars – purple

roze – pink

turquoise – turquoise

zwart – black

You now know enough colors to buy anything in any color you like, from T-shirts to cars and anything in between. If the color is not quite the same, you can add "-achtig" or "-ig" like the English language has -ish. So, a dress is "groenachtig" or "groenig" (greenish). A car may be "grijzig," "bruinig," or "zwartachtig."

Articles and Nouns/Pronouns

Now some more serious stuff. For many foreigners, the *articles* are a mystery they never solve. If it is any comfort, though, very few Dutch people know the exact grammar rules... Yet there are some simple rules for the articles:

The – **de** "duh" OR **het** "hèttt"

A or an – **een** "eyn"

To start with the easy part: **een** is used for every singular noun.

Then you have **de** and **het**: **de** is used for all male and female nouns. Yes, Dutch has male and female words, or at least they used to because nowadays, this distinction is not made anymore.

The article **het** is used for neutral words. Dutch has several—not countless, but still. You cannot tell whether a word is neutral or not, except for one kind of word: *the diminutives.* Whether that goes for male or female or neutral words, they are all treated the same: they get **het** as an article.

For plurals, the article is always **de**.

For instance:

The boy - **de** jongen "youngèn;" the little boy - **het** jongetje "youngetjuh"

The woman - **de** vrouw "vrau;" the little woman - **het** vrouwtje "vrautjuh"

The house - **het** huis "hoeys;" the little house - **het** huisje "hoeysjuh"

The boys - **de** jongens; the women - **de** vrouwen

So, how will you know when to use **het,** apart from the diminutives? Simple—you learn these words by heart. Here are a few of them you will use regularly:

bed - bed; **gebouw** - building "gggeboeyww;" **gras** - grass "gggras;" **huis** - house "hoeys;" **kind** - child "kint;" **lichaam** - body "licham;" **oog** - eye "oogg;" **oor** - ear "ohrr;" **schip** - ship "sggggip;" **vliegtuig** - plane "fleegggtoeyggg;" **zand** - sand "zantt."

Nouns

In Dutch, you call a noun *zelfstandig naamwoord*. Looks like a tongue twister? Don"t worry—you will not use this term in your day-to-day conversations. Nouns are all the words you use to describe an object, a person, a situation...

house - huis, mother - moeder, at work - aan het werk.

huis "hoeys;" moeder "muderrr;" werk "werk"

Pronouns

A pronoun is called *voornaamwoord* in Dutch. Pronouns have the same function as their English counterparts: indicating a specific object or person or referring to a person or object you mentioned before.

Pronouns in Dutch are **het, dit** and **dat** (it, this, and that). Indeed, **het** plays a role here as well! Quite a multitasker...

The pronouns often replace a certain noun. They refer to the word that means something that was mentioned before...

For instance, when you talk about a festival, you name the festival and the place where it is held. Then you can say: "**It** started last Saturday..." - "it" meaning: the festival.

Dutch does the same: they talk about the festival, where it is held, and then say: "**Het** begon zaterdag" (it started on Saturday)

Continue talking about the festival... and then you say: "This is more fun than the Efteling (Dutch theme park)" (**Dit** is leuker dan de Efteling)

By doing so, you avoid saying "festival" every two or three sentences. Check this in your own language. You do the same without really noticing it.

Mary has done some research. Hers is a lot better than **that** by Peter.

Mary heeft wat onderzoek gedaan. **Dat** van haar is veel beter dan **dat** van Peter.

Thus, avoiding repeating the word "onderzoek" - "research" ...

You also have, of course, the **personal pronouns,** which can be changed into several forms: the subject, the indirect object, or the possessive pronoun.

Here they are in a row:

Pers. Pronoun (**1**)/ subject (**2**)/ indirect object (**3**)/ possessive pronoun (**4**)

      1.   **2.**   **3.**   **4.**

I: ik - mij/me - mij/me - mijn

you: jij/je - jou/je - jou/je - jouw /u - u - u - uw

he: hij - hem - hem - zijn

she: zij - haar - haar - haar

we: wij/we - ons - ons - ons/onze (p)

you: jullie - jullie - jullie - jullie /u - u - u - uw

they: zij - hen - hen - hun

ik geef jou mijn boek (I give you my book)

ik – personal pronoun, jou – indirect object, mijn boek – subject, mijn – possessive pronoun

or

Ik geef mijn boek aan jou – in this case "aan jou" is the indirect object

NOTE: The Dutch also have a personal pronoun for people you don't know and are supposed to be polite to. In English, both forms are "you," but in Dutch, they have the polite personal pronoun "u." This "u" is conjugated the same way as "jij" in singular and as you – jullie in plural.

The only exception is when you are asking a question. If you ask a "je" question, you say, "**drink** jij veel water?" (Do you drink a lot of water?) When you talk to an older or unknown person, you ask, "**drinkt** u veel water?" (Do you drink a lot of water?) Then you give the u-form a "t" at the end of the verb.

Examples:

Hoe gaat het met u? – How are you?

Hebt u honger? – Are you hungry?

U hebt mooi gezongen! – You sang beautifully!

Drinkt u vaak wijn? – Do you drink wine often?

Of course, there are some exceptions to the rule—as always—but you will get to know them.

!OOPS!

You may have noticed some words that are written with two or three vowels after another, but not the same ones. Dutch has several:

au, eu, oe, ui, ou, oei

Of course, there is a way to pronounce them; otherwise, the Dutch language wouldn't have these glued vowels. Foreigners can find it hard to pronounce them correctly, though. It depends where you are from since Dutch is not the only language with difficult pronunciations. Again, don't worry—you will get the hang of it!

Au – "ahw" > > bl**au**w – blue "blahww"

Ou – "ahw" >> fout – mistake "fahwt"

Eu – "Ø"   > > d**eu**r – door "dØr"

Oe – "u"   > > m**oe** – tired "mu"

Ui – "oey" > > huis – house "hoeys"

Oei – "uj" > > knoei – spill "knuj"

Ohh... there is a little mean thing in these vowels! Have you spotted it? The Dutch have both "au" and "ou," and their pronunciation is the same! Why do they do that? Well... it just is what it is. Centuries of writing, spelling, and grammar are all mixed into the current language. Also, remember: You learn Dutch to speak Dutch, not to write a thesis in Dutch. Since both glued vowels are pronounced the same, do not worry about it.

Tiny task #2:

If you live in an area where Dutch words are everywhere, try to find ten Dutch words with these double vowels, write them down, learn how to pronounce them, and look up what they mean.

END OF !OOPS!

Now that you know a bit about pronouns, you have a list of the sorts of pronouns Dutch has. You will also notice it has grammatically the same pronouns as the English language:

The *demonstrative pronoun*: die & dat – this & that

Ik vind **die** jurk in **dat** patroon leuk – I like **this** dress in **that** pattern

The *relative pronoun*: die & dat

de auto, **die** te koop staat, ziet er geweldig uit – The car, the one **that** is for sale, looks great

The *indefinite pronoun*: iedere, elke, alle – each/every, all

Elke dag is anders – **Each** day is different

The *personal pronoun:*

I am not crazy; you are! – **Ik** ben niet gek; **jullie** zijn gek

The *exclamatory pronoun:* Wat – what

Wat een mooie dag! – **What** a beautiful day!

The *interrogative pronoun* – wie, welk, wat – who, what, what

Welke bloemen ga je plukken? – **What** flowers will you pick?

The *reflexive pronoun* – singular: me, je, zich; plural: ons, je, zich

Ik heb **me** niet gerealiseerd dat je gewond was – **I** did not realize you were hurt

Whenever a verb indicates it has something to do with the person speaking or described, the Dutch use this reflexive pronoun:

Ik zal **me** opfrissen en met je meegaan – I will freshen up and come with you

Hij moet **zich** schamen – He should be ashamed of himself

The *reciprocal pronoun:* elkaar – each other

We ontmoeten **elkaar** voor de bioscoop – We will meet each other in front of the cinema

Tiny task #3:

Can you make three sentences of every pronoun from the list above? With the examples given, it should not be too hard...

Prepositions

Prepositions (in Dutch: *voorzetsels*) are related to a noun. They are a group of words with a noun in it. They usually are put before the noun. Here are some examples of prepositions:

op (on), **voor** (in front of), **bij** (near), **achter** (behind), **door** (through), **in** (in), **aan** (at/on), **onder** (under)

Het boek ligt **op** de bank – The book is on the sofa

De bal viel **achter** het hek – The ball fell behind the gate

het kind slaapt **onder** het laken – The child sleeps under the sheet

And so on...

Adjectives

You know, of course, that you can make conversations as flowery as you like. With adjectives, you can describe something you love or hate and everything in between. However, when you talk to Dutch people, you will find they are quite down to earth. They like to call a spade a spade, without too much fuss about it. This does not mean they are rude... oh no! But they are not so "flowery" when they describe something or someone. Unless, of course, you talk to a poet!

To describe someone or something, you put the adjective before the noun—simple. Here are some examples:

de **rode** auto – the red car

de **ronde** tafel – the round table

de **dronken** vrouw – the drunk woman

het **hoge** gebouw – the tall building

het **groene** gras – the green grass

de **zilveren** ring – the silver ring

Now go a step further in the description:

de **mooie rode** auto – the beautiful red car

That is two for the price of one!

This way you can build quite a description. However, do not take it too far. As mentioned, the Dutch like it straight forward. If you think of more adjectives describing the car, people might think there is something fishy about it...

Tiny task #4:

Now form some Dutch sentences with what you just learned. Write down ten simple sentences with: an article, a noun, an adjective, and a preposition. Keep it simple, no verbs yet! For instance:

A nice book under the sofa – wow, two articles, two nouns, one adjective, and one preposition! Bingo!

Ten sentences in Dutch, of course... (Suggestion: Feel free to look up words in the dictionary that don't come to mind).

Part 2 – Grammar

Basic Dutch Verbs

No sentence is complete without a verb, and by using real, correct, and simple constructions, with one or two verbs in them, you will begin to *show off* your knowledge!

For starters:

zijn – to be

hebben – to have

These two verbs are the hardest to learn since they are irregular in the present tense. The remaining verbs will be a piece of cake.

ZIJN ("zɛin") to be

Singular: (S)

ik ben – I am

jij/u bent – you are

hij/zij/het is – he/she/it is

Plural: (P)

wij zijn – we are

jullie zijn – you are

zij zijn – they are

HEBBEN ("hɛbən") to have

Singular: (S)

ik heb – I have

jij/u hebt – you have

hij/zij/het heeft – he/she/it has

Plural: (P)

wij hebben – we have

jullie hebben – you have

zij hebben – they have

WILLEN ("willɛn") – to want

Singular: (S)

Ik wil – I want

Jij/ u wil – you want

Hij/zij/het wil – he/she/it wants

Plural: (P)

Wij willen – we want

Jullie willen – you want

Zij willen – they want

There is little to explain about the two verbs ZIJN and HEBBEN. WILLEN it is a bit different since "jij," "u," and "he/she/it" in singular DON'T get a -t. It's just a matter of learning these three verbs by heart, which is not that difficult.

The rest of the basic verbs are easy to compose once you know how to do it. Each verb has a so-called **root**, which is simple to find:

Lachen – to laugh – root = lach, so the -en is dropped.

Now that you have the root of lach, you can conjugate the verb lachen:

Ik lach –

Jij/u lacht – t

Hij/zij/het lacht – t

Wij lachen – en

Jullie lachen – en

Zij lachen – en

Summary: -nothing, -t, -t, -en, -en, -en

Easy? Yes!

Drinken – to drink – root = drink (drop the -en)

Here we go:

ik drink –

jij drinkt – t

hij/zij/het drinkt – t

wij drinken – en

jullie drinken – en

Zij drinken – en

Kijken – to look/watch – root = kijk

Fill in the conjugation yourself.

Some examples:

bedoelen – to mean

bouwen – to build

branden – to burn

drinken – to drink

huilen – to cry

poetsen – to clean

kijken – to look/to watch

lachen – to laugh

rijden – to drive

vloeien – to flow

voeren – to feed

wandelen – to stroll

Tiny task #5:

Can you conjugate all these Dutch verbs? If so, you are already doing great...

Here are some verbs that are conjugated in the same way, but have a *tiny thing* to pay attention to:

Eten – to eat – root = **eet**

Ik eet, jij eet, hij/zij/het eet, wij eten, jullie eten, zij eten

Slapen – to sleep – root = **slaap**

Ik slaap, jij slaapt, hij/zij/het slaapt, wij slapen, jullie slapen, zij slapen

Did you notice that the root and the conjugations in the singular are slightly different? The plural is easy, though. These are all verbs with one vowel in the verb. The root gets two vowels, to prevent the verb from getting a totally different meaning (in some cases) or making it hard to pronounce.

Here are some verbs you will regularly encounter in Dutch conversations:

dromen – to dream – root = droom

eten – to eat – root = eet

koken – to cook – root = kook

lopen – to walk – root = loop

menen – to mean – root = meen

slapen – to sleep – root = slaap

spelen – to play – root = speel

NOTE: Only the singular uses the root indicated. The plural uses the same old way: wij lopen; wij koken; wij menen, etc. Simple as that!

There are also verbs with a *tiny different* thing to pay attention to:

wassen – to wash – root = was (drop one consonant)

plassen – to pee – root = plas

krabben – to scratch – root = krab

leggen – to place – root = leg

Plus:

lezen – to read – root = lees (one extra e; z changes into s)

schrijven – to write – root = schrijf (change v into f)

Did you notice that the plural is the same as the original verb: wij wassen; wij krabben; wij lezen, etc.?

And there are other verbs with, again, a *tiny different* thing to pay attention to:

gaan – to go – root = ga (drop one vowel + n) – plural: wij gaan

slaan – to hit – root = sla – plural: wij slaan

staan – to stand – root = sta – plural: wij staan

Did you notice that the plural of these verbs is the same as the verb itself: wij/jullie/zij staan?

You do not have to be a language expert to learn how these different kinds of verbs should be handled. Once you see the logic of it—and there is a logic—you will easily master the use of them. Besides that, it is a matter of learning by heart, step by step...

Below, the above verbs have been listed alphabetically, so you can now use them in a conversation!

bedoelen – to mean

bouwen – to build

branden – to burn

drinken – to drink

dromen – to dream – root = droom (root gets two vowels)

eten – to eat – root = eet (root gets two vowels)

gaan – to go – root = ga (drop one vowel + n) – plural: wij gaan

huilen – to cry

kijken – to look/to watch

komen – to come – root = kom

koken – to cook – root = kook

krabben – to scratch – root = krab

lachen – to laugh

leggen – to place – root = leg (drop one consonant)

lopen – to walk – root = loop (root gets two vowels)

lezen – to read – root = lees (one extra e; z changes into s)

menen – to mean – root = meen (root gets 2 vowels)

plassen – to pee – root = plas (drop one consonant)

schrijven – to write – root = schrijf (change v into f)

slaan – to hit – root = sla – plural: wij slaan

slapen – to sleep – root = slaap (root gets two vowels)

spelen – to play – root = speel (root gets two vowels)

staan – to stand – root = sta – plural: wij staan

rijden – to drive

vloeien – to flow

voeren – to feed

wandelen – to stroll

wassen – to wash – root = was (drop one consonant)

If you like statistics: This list contains 28 verbs for everyday use, apart from "hebben," "willen," and "zijn,"—these three are used so often that you will lose track. Together, that is 31 verbs! If you feel like learning them by heart, you are welcome to do so. It would certainly help you moving forward...

Time to make some sentences that make sense!

Now that you have mastered a lot of verbs, you can use them in a logical Dutch sentence.

To construct sentences, you must take notice of the normal word order in Dutch. In simple sentences, the order is simple as well:

subject, verb, object: ik lees een boek

or: subject, verb, adjective, object: ik lees een mooi boek

Hij drinkt een kopje thee – He drinks (is drinking) a cup of tea

Wij kijken samen televisie – We watch (are watching) television together

Ik heb een nieuw boek – I have a new book

Jullie komen hier vaak – You come here often

Zij is heel serieus – She is very serious

Wij zijn heel tevreden – We are very satisfied

Jij speelt geweldig piano – You play the piano marvelously

Hij is een slechte kok – He is a bad cook

Ik droom bijna elke nacht – I dream almost every night

Het huis brandt helemaal af – The house burns down completely

Tiny task #6:

Below are some nouns, adjectives, articles, and verbs for you to construct Dutch sentences with. You can make one sentence/conjugation with each line, or conjugate the whole verb!

Eten – maaltijd – hij – lekkere – een

Planten – bloemen – wij – allerlei

Lezen – krant – jij – een – goede

Wassen – kleren – ik – vuile

Drinken – thee - zij (s) – warme

Strijken – overhemd – jullie – het – blauwe

Schrijven – lange – brief – ik – een

Geven – cadeau – klein – jij – een

Hebben   hond - zij (p) – grote – een

Kopen – schoenen – ik – nieuwe

Okay, how did that go? Easy? Or did you spend way too much time trying to form nice short sentences? It is all a matter of practice, of course. Practice makes perfect, so do not despair if this did not quite go according to your expectation... You will get there!

Vocabulary – miscellaneous

afbranden – to burn down

allerlei – all kinds of

bijna – almost

de bloem* – flower

het boek – book

de brief – letter

het cadeau – present/gift

dromen – to dream

geven – to give

geweldig – marvelous

goed – good/well

groot – big/large

heel – very

heel – whole

hier – here

de hond – dog

klein – small

de kleren – clothes

de kok – cook

de kop – cup

het kopje – small cup

de krant – newspaper

lang – long

lekker – nice/tasty

lezen – to read

de maaltijd – meal

mooi – beautiful

de nacht – night

nieuw – new

het overhemd – shirt

de piano – piano

planten – to plant

de plant – plant/shrub

samen – together

de schoen – shoe

schrijven – to write

slecht – bad

strijken – to iron

de televisie – television

tevreden – satisfied/happy

de thee – tea

vaak – often

vuil – dirty

wassen – to wash

For your convenience, the articles "de" and "het" have been out before any noun in the vocabularies. Also, leave them out in the English translation, as they are all the same! This way, you learn the various articles as you go, without making too much of a fuss about it.

!OOPS!

So far, you have encountered a **whole lot of words and verbs.** If you organize those words for yourself, such as in a notebook, by going over the pages, you learn them simultaneously.

Writing things down has a funny consequence. By writing the words in a notebook, your brain does two things at once. It sees the word you are copying and takes notice of it, AND while you are writing the word down, it takes notice of it again! So, your brain actually *sees* the word twice, which makes it easier for you to remember.

Have you ever made a shopping list before going to the supermarket or grocery store? And then left the list at home? Well, as it turns out, you still remember about 80 percent of what you wrote on the list when you are loading your shopping basket. How come? You wrote everything down!

Summary: The more you write down, the easier you remember!

NOTE: The brain really likes to be busy... Scientific research shows that the more your brain must do, the better and longer it stays intact. Lazy brains can be activated at any time and any age. A busy brain at an old/older age is a thing to cherish, so start *working out* that brain of yours!

END OF !OOPS!

Modal Verbs

The world of verbs is a big one! Just as you thought you were well on your way, you get another type of verb to tackle... But you will be fine. Once you know these few **modal verbs**, you will be able to form many more sentences that will impress every Dutch person you meet. And one other thing—it is not very hard to master...

Many verbs need something extra. For instance, if you need to see a doctor, you can say: "I go to the doctor." However, you do not go there *voluntarily*; you go because there is a medical problem. So, the correct sentence would be: "I **have to** go to the doctor." In Dutch, that would be: "Ik **moet** naar de dokter (gaan)."

The modal verb is a little helper, an *auxiliary verb*. It helps express more accurately what you want to say. The modal verbs in Dutch are:

hoeven, kunnen, moeten, mogen, willen, zullen

hoeven – to need/want/like – root = hoef

kunnen – to can/be able/be possible – root = kan

moeten – to have/ought/should to/to must – root = moet

mogen – to may/to like/have the right/are allowed – root = mag

willen – to want/desire/wish/shall – root = wil

zullen – to shall/ought to/will – root = zal

In Dutch, you put the modal verb at the beginning of a sentence. The infinitive verb comes at the end of the sentence. Like this:

ik **kan** nooit op zaterdag **komen** – I can never come on Saturdays

jij **mag** met je speelgoed **spelen** – you may play with your toys

wij **moeten** boodschappen **doen** – we have to run some errands/we have to shop for groceries

zij **wil** concertkaartjes kopen – she wants to buy tickets for the concert hij **zal** morgen even **komen** – he will come by tomorrow

jij **hoeft*** niet te **koken** – you don't need to cook

*the verb **hoeven** is only used in denials. *Mind the v change into an f!*

The conjugation of these verbs is, in a few cases, like the normal verbs. This goes for the modal verbs:

moeten and hoeven

For the other verbs, the conjugation is a bit different:

kunnen – ik kan, jij **kunt**, hij/zij/het **kan**, wij/jullie/zij kunnen

mogen – ik mag, jij **mag**, hij/zij/het **mag**, wij/jullie/zij mogen

willen – ik wil, jij **wil**, hij/zij/het **wil**, wij/jullie/zij willen

zullen – ik zal, jij **zult**, hij/zij/het **zal**, wij/jullie/zij willen

Verbs in a Question

The Dutch language has exceptions, just like any other language. One very important exception is the verb in a question when **jij** is involved. Then, the conjugation changes.

What happens? The **-t** will be left out; that is, if there is a -t to start with. For example:

Jij loopt naar school – **loop jij** naar school?

Jij droomt elke nacht – **droom jij** wel eens?

For all verbs or auxiliary verbs, the direct verb is placed first, then the subject. The same applies in English:

Will *you* come to the cinema?   – Ga *je* mee naar de bioscoop?

Do *you* eat meat very often? – Eet *jij* vaak vlees?

Are *they* staying at home alone? – Blijven *zij* alleen thuis?

Does *he* wash his own clothes? – Wast *hij* zijn eigen kleren?

You may notice that the English language often uses an auxiliary verb to ask a question. In Dutch, you go straight to what you want to know... As mentioned, Dutch people are quite direct in their language. There is no fuss—just say what you have to/want to say.

Tiny Task #7:

Remember the ten sentences you made with articles, adjectives, nouns, and verbs? Good! Now, get those sentences and put them in question form! Write them down again, keeping in mind what was said earlier about that busy brain of yours...

Tenses

There is no use getting tense over tenses. Every language has them, and Dutch is no different. When you can use the tenses correctly, you are on the way up!

So, it is time to tackle these tenses, which have a certain logic to them—and for the ones that don't, it's just a matter of learning as you go.

Simple past tense

So far, you have only used the present tense.

Now, you continue with the **simple past tense**. You use the past tense to describe something that happened in the past. In Dutch, the simple past tense is called: *onvoltooid verleden tijd (ovt)*. Yes, it is quite a mouthful, so the abbreviation **ovt** is used.

Simple past tense - ovt

For all the verbs that you have learned, you first had to identify the root. That goes for the ovt as well.

The regular verbs:

Lachen - root = lach - ovt = lach**te**/lach**ten**

Ik/jij/hij/zij/het lach**te** - wij/jullie/zij lach**ten**

Duwen - root = duw - ovt = duw**de**/duw**den**

Ik/jij/hij/zij/het duw**de** – wij/jullie/zij duw**den**

Simple. Right? Just add **-te** or **-ten** to the root, or **-de** or **-den**.

Ah, but what do you see? Some verbs end in **-te** in the ovt and others end in **-de**! Correct. The reason for that has to do with pronunciation. Rest assured: Most verbs have -de in the ovt, but a handful has -te. However, many Dutch people misuse these two forms, especially in the past participle—which will be detailed shortly.

For now, you will learn an old trick to help you deduce what verbs get a **-t** in the ovt and the past participle...

It is called **K O F S C H I P.**

This is a word without any meaning—a word for a trick. Skip the vowels o and i and you have **KFSCHP.** The verbs with the root ending in one of these letters or a combination of them (ch) get a **t** in the ovt and the past participle. Easy...

Examples:

kussen – to kiss – root = kus – ovt: ku**ste**

pakken – to get – root = pak – ovt: pa**kte**

wippen – to hop – root = wip – ovt: wi**pte**

blaffen – to bark – root = blaf – ovt: bla**fte**

coachen – to coach – root = coach – ovt: coa**chte**

The conjugation of these verbs in ovt is the same as with verbs that have -de in ovt:

ik kuste, jij kuste, hij/zij kuste, wij/jullie/zij kusten

Tiny task #8:

Write down the past tense (ovt) of these ten verbs (Tip: Look up the verbs you don't recognize):

koken; wonen; fietsen; rollen; draaien; fotograferen; graaien; lachen; sjouwen; drinken

Irregular verbs

There is no escape possible! The Dutch language also has irregular verbs—as most languages do. And when it comes to the irregulars, there is no sense in looking for a meaningful explanation. It is what it is. Therefore, you must learn them by heart.

(Tip: Write down five irregular verbs on a piece of paper and peek at any time. If you review them several times a day, you should remember them the next day. Once you remember them, great! Move on and write five more down on a piece of paper, and so on. If you can't manage to name all five, just give it an extra day! Take your time—you will master them!)

NOTE: The list below is not complete; only verbs used in a normal Dutch conversation have been included. The *past participle (pp)* has also been added, of which will be detailed shortly...

The three major verbs:

zijn – to be – ik/jij/hij/zij was; wij/jullie/zij waren
    was/waren/geweest (= pp)

hebben – to have – ik/jij/hij/zij had; wij/jullie/zij hadden
    had/hadden/gehad

worden – to be (will be) – ik/jij/hij/zij werd; wij/jullie/zij werden
    werd/werden/geworden

Now it is continued alphabetically (Tip: Look up the verbs you don't recognize):

A

B

brengen – bracht/brachten/gebracht; bedriegen – bedroog/bedrogen/bedrogen; blijven – bleef/bleven/gebleven; bidden – bad/baden/gebeden; bijten – beet/beten/gebeten; binden – bond/bonden/gebonden; blazen – blies/bliezen/geblazen; breken –

brak/braken/gebroken; beginnen - begon/begonnen/begonnen; buigen - boog/bogen/gebogen;

C

D

drinken - dronk/dronken/gedronken; denken - dacht/dachten/gedacht; dragen - droeg/droegen/gedragen; duiken - dook/doken/gedoken;

E

eten - at/aten/gegeten;

F

fluiten - floot/floten/gefloten;

G

genezen - genas/genazen/genezen; geven - gaf/gaven/gegeven; genieten - genoot/genoten/genoten; gieten - goot/goten/gegoten; grijpen - greep/grepen/gegrepen; glimmen - glom/glommen/geglommen;

H

houden (van) - hield/hielden (van)/gehouden; helpen - hielp/hielpen/geholpen; hangen - hing/hingen/gehangen

I

J

jagen - joeg/joegen/gejaagd;

K

klimmen - klom/klommen/geklommen; komen - kwam/kwamen/gekomen; kiezen - koos/kozen/gekozen; kijken - keek/keken/gekeken; knijpen - kneep/knepen/geknepen; kruipen - kroop/kropen/gekropen; klinken - klonk/klonken/geklonken;

L

lopen – liep/liepen/gelopen; liegen – loog/logen/gelogen; lezen – las/lazen/gelezen; liggen – lag/lagen/gelegen; lijken – leek/leken/geleken;

M

moeten – moest/moesten/gemoeten; meten – mat/maten/gemeten;

N

nemen – nam/namen/genomen;

O

P

prijzen – prees/prezen/geprezen;

R

ruiken – rook/roken/geroken; roepen – riep/riepen/geroepen; rijden – reed/reden/gereden;

S

slapen – sliep/sliepen/geslapen; schenken – schonk/schonken/geschonken; schieten – schoot/schoten/geschoten; schrijven – schreef/schreven/geschreven; spreken – sprak/spraken/gesproken; schrikken – schrok/schrokken/geschrokken; stelen – stal/stalen/gestolen; smelten – smolt/smolten/gesmolten; spijten – speet/speten/gespeten; springen – sprong/sprongen/gesprongen; sterven – stierf/stierven/gestorven; stinken – stonk/stonken/gestonken;

T

trekken – trok/trokken/getrokken;

U

V

vergeten – vergat/vergaten/vergeten; vragen – vroeg/vroegen/gevraagd; vallen – viel/vielen/gevallen; verliezen – verloor/verloren/verloren; vinden – vond/vonden/gevonden; vliegen – vloog/vlogen/gevlogen; vangen – ving/vingen/gevangen;

W

winnen – won/wonnen/gewonnen; weten – wist/wisten/geweten; wegen – woog/wogen/gewogen; wijzen – wees/wezen/gewezen;

Z

zwijgen – zweeg/zwegen/gezwegen; zien – zag/zagen/gezien; zingen – zong/zongen/gezongen; zwemmen – zwom/zwommen/gezwommen; zeggen – zei/zeiden/gezegd; zitten – zat/zaten/gezeten; zoeken – zocht/zochten/gezocht;

Quite a list, right? And that is not even half of the irregular verbs, roughly speaking. However, these verbs are a great start. You will certainly encounter other irregular verbs once you get to talk regularly with Dutch people. If you do, try to write them down with the correct forms (ask for them) and add them to your list of verbs!

Past participle

You have seen the present tense and past tense, so now you continue with the **past participle (pp)**. In Dutch, this is called *voltooid deelwoord.* "Voltooid" meaning "done." After all, once you have done something, it is done! Dutch has regular pp's and—of course—irregular pp's. Here are the regular ones:

The past principle is formed by putting **ge-** in front of the past tense in singular and dropping the **-e** at the end:

werken – werk**te** (s) – **ge**werkt = have worked

duwen – duw**de** (s) –   **ge**duw**d** = have pushed

The auxiliary verb used for the past principle is "hebben" (to have) or "zijn" (to be). The auxiliary verb "hebben" is used most often... You conjugate that verb and the pp is the same for all conjugations.

ik **heb geknipt** - I have cut

jij **hebt gehuild** - you have cried

zij **heeft gewandeld** - she has strolled

hij **heeft gewerkt** - he has worked

wij **hebben geduwd** - we have pushed

jullie **hebben gedanst** - you have danced

zij **hebben gekookt** - they have cooked

Basically, it is simple to do—once you know how. If you make mistakes with the -t or -d at the end of the pp, keep in mind that most Dutch people do, too. That is, most young Dutch people, up to thirty (or even a bit older). Why? This is one explanation:

In the "olden" days, roughly 40 to 50 years ago, the Dutch were taught how to spell with the trick word: KOFSCHIP. They swore by it, and then, at a certain point, they didn't need the trick word anymore—they were just doing it out of habit.

Then, suddenly, the trick word was not used anymore. This perhaps occurred at the same time pocket calculators entered the classrooms... And what happened? The kids at school could not spell as well.

You think that correct spelling is part of your education. Nowadays, though, you stand out if you send in a *correctly* written letter or resume. The *you* in this book clearly comes from the "olden" days!

Another explanation could be that correct spelling is not so "hip" anymore. If you get the meaning of what people want to say, don't whine over a misspelled word or grammatical mistake. The message comes through, doesn't it? It is the same with the calculators—who cares if kids cannot count, subtract or add up properly anymore?

There are calculators, computers, and plenty of software to help them out.

Do you want to terribly confuse a young cashier? Ask him or her when you pay, e.g., the item is $15.30 and you give a note of $20, "Shall I add 30 cents?" The poor cashier will get totally flustered and think: *What the heck do you mean?* His or her cash register will tell them to return $4.70—don't mess with the money or the software!

There is a bit more to learn about the past particle. Remember that Dutch has irregular verbs... which also goes for the past particle. In the list of the irregular verbs, both the past tense and past particle were included. Scroll up and you will see them again. You have probably been memorizing them without realizing it. If so, well done! If not, you have got your verbs cut out for you...

As mentioned, the auxiliary verb is usually "hebben," except when that sounds strange. E.g., groeien (to grow) – groeide – ik **heb** gegroeid = wrong. It is "ik **ben** gegroeid." Growing is something you yourself cannot influence.

Here are a few examples:

zijn – was – ik ben geweest

worden – werd – ik ben geworden

beginnen – begon – we zijn begonnen

vallen – viel – ik ben gevallen

bijten – beet – ik ben gebeten

There are also verbs in which you can use both auxiliaries. BUT they have a different meaning, which you will see in these examples:

bijten – beet –	ik **heb** gebeten – I am active, I bite in an apple
	Ik **ben** gebeten – I am passive, a dog bit me, or an insect

bedriegen – bedroog	ik **heb** bedrogen – I am actively cheating (friend, partner)
	Ik **ben** bedrogen – I am passive, I was cheated on
vergeten – vergat	Ik **heb** vergeten – I did not do all I was planning to
	Ik **ben** vergeten – nobody remembers me

With "vergeten," people tend to use "ik ben vergeten" when they forgot to do something. Although it is technically wrong, it's generally accepted nowadays.

verliezen – verloren	ik **heb** verloren – I lost something
	Ik **ben** verloren – I am lost. Nothing can save me anymore
vinden – vond	ik **heb** gevonden – I found something
	ik **ben** gevonden – they found me, when I was lost
knijpen – kneep	ik **heb** geknepen – I pinched someone, or something
	ik **ben** geknepen – someone pinched me, it hurts

This is not a thorough list of all the verb possibilities. These are just a few examples to show you that you must sometimes think twice before you use an auxiliary. For the real language knacks, it is fun to find more verbs that have a double meaning. For everyone else, it is just another fact to deal with when mastering Dutch.

Vocabulary – Some Extra Verbs (both in the text above ↑ and in the text below ↓ from here...)

bedriegen – to cheat

beginnen – to begin/to start

behandelen – to treat

bijten – to bite

dansen – to dance

duwen – to push

eten – to eat

knippen – to cut

knijpen – to pinch

koken – to cook

scheren – to shave

slapen – to sleep

vallen – to fall

vergeten – to forget

verliezen – to lose

vinden – to find

werken – to work

Tiny task #9

Write down ten Dutch sentences in which you use the past participle, with the auxiliary verb "hebben." Then write five sentences using the past participle with the auxiliary verb "zijn."

When you are done, give yourself a compliment for writing and knowing so much Dutch already! Try to talk as much as possible and don't forget: Practice makes perfect!

Past perfect

The past perfect is not hard to learn; it is quite simple. You use the verb "hebben" in the simple past as an auxiliary verb and the past particle.

Like this:

Ik **heb** al gegeten – I have eaten already (present)

Ik **had** al gegeten – I had eaten already (past)

Ik **heb** lekker geslapen – I have slept well (present)

Ik **had** lekker geslapen – I had slept well (past)

Etc. That is it!

Passive form

Dutch also uses the passive form of many verbs. These verbs indicate something is "happening" to you, him, us. If you want, you can transform these sentences into active ones, but sometimes passive is the best way to go.

Example:

Ik **word behandeld** voor xxxx – I am being treated for xxxx

Ik **ben behandeld** voor xxxx   – I have been treated for xxxx

Ik **word geschoren** – I am being shaved

Ik **ben geschoren** – I have been shaved

As you can see, the verbs "worden" and "hebben" are being used. They are auxiliary verbs for what you really mean to say: I am being **treated.** That is what you want to tell someone else. And for that, you need a few verbs.

Since you are "being treated," here are some common ailments, terms, and phrases:

Vocabulary – Ailments

de buikpijn – bellyache, stomachache

de hoest – cough

hoesten – to cough

de hoofdpijn – headache

de keelpijn – throat ache

de kiespijn – toothache

de migraine – migraine

misselijk – nauseous

de oorpijn – earache

overgeven – to throw up, to vomit

de pijn – hurt, ache

de rugpijn – back pain

ziek – ill, sick

pijn in: – pain in:

enkel – ankle

de borst – chest

de hand – hand

de heup – hip

de knie – knee

de vinger – finger

de voet – foot

Ik heb daar al eerder last van gehad – I had problems with that before

Ik ben daarvoor behandeld – I have been treated for that

Het is erger dan gisteren – It is worse than yesterday

Ik heb dat elk jaar een paar keer – I have this a few times a year

debronchitis –bronchitis

Ik ben zwanger – I am pregnant

hoge bloeddruk – high blood pressure

Ik ben hartpatiënt – I am a heart patient

Ik heb diabetes – I have diabetes

Ik kan moeilijk ademhalen – I have difficulty breathing

deastma – asthma

Ik ben longpatient – I am a lung patient

Ik ben allergisch voor xxx: =–I am allergic to xxx:

de allergie: – allergy:

de antibiotica – antibiotics

bloemen – flowers

huisdieren – pets

hete peper – hot pepper

de jodium – iodine

de penicilline – penicillin

pollen – pollen

het stof – dust

vogels – birds

de wol – wool

Vocabulary – Healthcare

de afspraak – appointment

het alarmnummer – emergency number

de ambulance – ambulance

de dokter – doctor

de pijnstiller – pain killer

het recept – prescription

terugkomen – return visit, follow-up visit

de verpleegkundige – nurse

spreekuur – office/consultation hours

de wachtkamer – waiting room

zonder recept – over the counter

Kan ik een recept krijgen? – Can I get a prescription?

Kan ik pijnstillers krijgen? – Can I get pain killers?

Kan ik dit zonder recept kopen? - Can I buy this over the counter?

Wanneer moet ik terugkomen? - When will you see me again?

Ik wil graag een afspraak maken - I would like to make an appointment

U kunt in de wachtkamer wachten - You can wait in the waiting room

Heeft de dokter een vrij spreekuur? - Does the doctor have office hours?

Bel een ambulance, snel! - Please, call an ambulance! Quickly!

Wilt u 112 bellen? - Please, call 112 (emergency number)

Snel, bel het alarmnummer! - Quickly! Call the emergency number!

112 Alarmnummer

112   Emergency number for the Netherlands

Part 3 – Conversation

It is time to practice everything that you have learned so far. Then, you can go out and meet some Dutch people to share your excellent new vocabulary with.

Informal

1 Hallo, goedemiddag. Mag ik twee bier van de tap?

2 Goedemiddag. Welke wil je?

3 Uh... doe maar Heineken/Amstel/Hertog Jan/Jupiler (whatever brand is on the knobs of the beer handles).

4 Twee bier. Alsjeblieft.

5 Dank je wel.

(Walk away from the bar and take a seat or stay near the bar and grab a bar stool.)

That was fun, wasn't it? But what did you do and say?

1 Hello, good afternoon. Can I get two beers from the tap?

2 Good afternoon. Which one would you like?

3 Uh... I would like a Heineken/Amstel, etc.

4 Two beers, here you go.

5 Thanks.

A similar conversation can also occur when you order coffee or wine.

Red wine - rode wijn

White wine - witte wijn >> dry wine - droge wijn

Rosé or pink wine - rosé wijn

Koffie - coffee

Cappuccinno - cappuccino

Now that you have your coffee or wine, you want to socialize. In small cafés, the patrons are open to chatting to strangers. You are clearly new, not a local, so they want to get to know you. In the more urban cafés, the grand cafés, and very modern cafés in the city center, people come in and have a drink to meet friends and coworkers. Their attention does not go to visitors who walk in and ask—in their best Dutch—for a drink. They go with the in-crowd, and you are definitely not one of them.

On the other hand, a hotel bar is a perfect place to socialize as well. Just beware of the nice, beautiful women in the bar of a big hotel. There is a fifty-fifty chance that they are not there to "chat" but to earn a living. Of course, you cannot bring up that topic, in case the beautiful woman is a hotel guest, just like you, or an innocent visitor. It is best is to avoid the "lonely ladies." Unless you have other plans, of course...

So, small cafés and hotel bars are some good places to practice the Dutch language.

You: Leuk café, dit - Nice café, this one

The other: Jahaa... best wel - Yeah... it's nice

You: Ik kom hier voor het eerst - This is my first time here

Other: Ah... dacht ik al... - Ah... I thought so

You: Ik ben hier xxx dagen/weken – I will be here for xxx days/weeks

Other: O ja?... goed zo, mooi – Really? Good, fine

You: Ik kom uit xxxxx – I am from xxxx

NOTE: If you come from a city that Dutch people might know, mention the city—like New York, Madrid, Barcelona, Londen, etc. If not, just mention your country.

Other: Oh. En hoe bevalt het hier? – Oh. And how do you like it here?

You: Prima. Leuke stad, mooi land – Just fine. Great city, beautiful country

Other: Ja, het is hier prima – Yes, the city is okay

Other: Ben je al in xxxxx geweest? – Have you been to xxxxx?

You: Ja, dat was prachtig!/Heel leuk – Yes. It was awesome/Very nice!

You: Nee, maar daar willen we wel heen – No, but we want to go there

You: Nee, daar hebben we helaas geen tijd voor – No, unfortunately, we don't have the time.

(Tip: Never talk negatively about a Dutch city, village, the country in general, or an attraction. The Dutch criticize everything and everybody, but no stranger or tourist is allowed to tell them something in their "beloved" country is not okay! You can have a different opinion, of course, but use discretion. Instead, just say something like, "It was very nice – het was (wel) leuk." Stay on a neutral subject and move on to discuss your plans while in the country, or what you have seen already that you enjoyed! That way your conversation will last a bit longer.)

Here, you may or may not shake hands. Remember, though, that you are in a small café, so formal manners are not required.

Other: Ik ben Karl, trouwens – My name is Karl, by the way

You: Dag, Karl. Leuk je te leren kennen. Ik heet Peter - Hi, Karl, nice to meet you. My name is Peter

You: Woon je hier in xxx? - Do you live here in xxxx?

Other: Jaaa, mijn hele leven al - Yeah, all my life.

You: Leuke plek om te wonen - Nice place to live

You: Wil je iets drinken? - Can I get you a drink?

NOTE: Only suggest this last question if you have enough money on you. Do not offer a drink and have an awkward situation afterward. If you happen to be short on cash or don't have a (credit) card on you, don't offer anything. However, only accept one drink from the other person. You do not want to give your new friend the impression that you are a freeloader...)

(Tip: Do not stretch the conversation if it is dragging. Dutch people in a café or bar tend to move around to chat with folks and friends loosely, no strings attached. So, let them go. If you like the ambiance, stay. If your thirst is quenched and you feel kind of lost, move on...)

If things go smoothly, you can talk about this or that by asking questions and sharing things about yourself. Do not make it an interrogation, though.

You: Is het hier altijd zo druk/zo rustig? - Is it always this crowded/quiet here?

Other: Naahh... meestal drukker/rustiger - Nah... usually more crowded/quieter

Other: Ja, zo is het hier meestal wel, ja - Yeah, this is the usual, yes

You: Elke dag? - Every day?

Other: Hm... drukker in het weekend - Hmm... more people on the weekend

You: Natuurlijk, dan zijn mensen vrij - Of course, people are off, then

Other: Yep! - Yep!

You: Ik werk in xxxx* – I work in the xxxx*

Other: Oh... goed, man! –Oh... right on, man!

You: En jij? Wat voor werk doe jij? – And you? What do you do?

*Here, mention your actual job, in general, but not in detail. If it is a job in a specific industry, just mention the industry, not the job itself.

Ik werk in – I work in:

de gezondheidszorg – health care

als – as a:

de arts – doctor

de laborant – lab assistant

de operatieassistent – operation assistant

de specialist – specialist

de verpleegkundige – nurse

de verzorger – caretaker, orderly

de autobranche – the car industry

Ik ben autodealer – I am a car dealer

In de fabriek – in the factory

Ik ben monteur – I am a mechanic

Ik ben verkoper – I am a salesperson

Notice that you use an "a" in English when you describe yourself or someone else? I am **a** salesperson... In Dutch, you do not do that. Just: "ik ben," "hij is," and then the description you want to give.

A few jobs/professions:

de accountant – accountant

de boekhouder – bookkeeper

de bouwvakker – construction worker

de consultant – consultant

het hotelkamermeisje – hotel maid

de leraar – teacher

de loodgieter – plumber

de officemanager – office manager

de receptionist – receptionist

de schilder – painter

de telefonist – phone operator

de timmerman – carpenter

And so on.

Once you are getting friendly, you can discuss the pros and cons of your job or profession. That also goes for the person you are talking with as well. That can give you something to chat about. If the job or profession is not worth talking about, you can change the subject.

Talking about sports might be an idea. Remember: The Dutch word for "soccer" is "voetbal." If you want to talk about football with your new Dutch friend, you speak of "rugby."

Some common sports in a handy list:

atletiek – athletics

honkbal – baseball

rugby – rugby/football

schaatsen – ice skating

tennis – tennis

voetbal – soccer

wielrennen – cycling

zwemmen – swimming

Be aware that most Dutch people are crazy about "voetbal." The country changes into an orange-colored world whenever the national soccer team participates in the European or World Championship. Banners, flags, crazy hats, funny hats, garlands, etc.—everything is orange and red-white-blue. Voetbal is serious business.

The same goes for ice skating. The Dutch have several fantastic skaters. Throughout the decades, people have been metaphorically glued to their television sets, so they never miss a race. Take notice because if you happen to know a bit about it, the Dutch will appreciate you even more!

NOTE: Why all this orange as the festive color? Well, as it happens, the kingdom of the Netherlands is ruled by The House of Oranje (Orange), a royal name that goes back for centuries. Besides the red/white/blue national flag, the Dutch also have an orange pennant. On national holidays, you can see both on official buildings, with the pennant flapping above the flag. Hence, all the orange when sports are getting "serious."

Then there are the cycling races. A few are very popular, but it is the Tour de France that really stands out. At the end of the afternoon, around 5:00 p.m., the cyclists reach the finish of that day's race. If you do not like cycling, then don't enter most cafés at that time. At around 6:00 p.m., you are safe as there are other popular races, like the Giro d'Italia and the Vuelta in Spain, but "de tour," as the Tour de France is fondly called, is at the top.

Talking about family is a good idea, too, once you get acquainted. The Dutch are not quick to show off their family, except for grandparents who always tend to carry pics of their grandkids. So be mildly modest with "digging" into the family of someone else.

Vocabulary – Family

de jongen – boy

de dochter – daughter

de familie – family

de grootouder – grandparent

het kind/de kinderen – child/children

het kleinkind – grandchild

het meisje – girl

de moeder – mother

de oma – grandmother

de oom – uncle

de opa – grandfather

de schoonfamilie – in-laws

de schoonmoeder/vader – mother/father-in-law

de schoonzus – sister-in-law

de tante – aunt

de vader – father

de zoon – son

de zwager – brother-in-law

Remember: Do not go into too much detail concerning a family tale, as you don't know the people you are talking with very well yet.

Formal

It is time to get more formal. Suppose you are going to meet one or more Dutch people for business. In this case, do not buy them a drink, dress appropriately (anything from smart casual to suit plus tie, which is contingent on where you are going), and behave politely. Depending on whether they need you or you need them, you act accordingly. There is a slight difference...

You enter a building and walk up to the reception desk:

You: Goedemorgen, ik heb een afspraak – Good morning, I have an appointment

Recep: Wat is uw naam? – May I have your name, please?

You: xxxx – xxxx

Recep: U hebt een afspraak met...? – Whom do you have an appointment with?

You: Met meneer/mevrouw xxxx – With Mr/Ms xxxxx

Recep: Oké, ik bel even – Okay, I will give them a call.

Recep: U kunt daar even wachten – You can wait over there

You: Dank u wel – Thank you

Some polite phrases can get you a long way...

Other: Alstublieft/alsjeblieft – Here you are

You: Dank u wel – Thank you

Other: Wilt u een kopje koffie of thee? – Would you like a cup of coffee/tea?

You: ja, graag/nee, dank u wel – Yes, please/no, thank you

Other: wilt u melk en suiker? – Do you want/take cream and sugar?

You: nee, dank u, ik drink het zwart – No, thank you, I'll have it black

You: ja graag/alleen melk/alleen suiker/allebei – Yes, please/just cream/just sugar/both

NOTE: A simple "ja" or "nee" when you are offered a drink, is not considered polite. Some countries or languages do it that way, but in Dutch, you add a few words...

Are you looking to get a job? Then you need your résumé, and some examples of your work if possible. Even if you already sent everything digitally, still bring a hard copy with you. That will make you look proactive, which Dutch people will respect.

In another scenario, say you walk with one or two people into an office. When invited, you sit down (and not beforehand!) and wait until the other party starts the conversation. No small talk on your part unless someone else initiates it.

Other: Fijn dat u kon komen, mevrouw xxx – Glad you could come, Ms xxxx

You: Geen probleem, fijn dat u me uitnodigde – No problem, I am glad you invited me

Other: Eens kijken... - Let me see...

Other: U hebt dit werk al vaker gedaan? - You have done this work before?

You: Ja, al een aantal jaren/al een paar keer - Yes, for several years/a few times

Other: Wat vindt u leuk aan dit werk? - What do you like about this job?

You: de zelfstandigheid/creativiteit/teamwork - The independence/creativity/ teamwork

You: Ik houd er van om... - I like to...

You: Samen te werken/alleen te werken - to work together/work on my own

You: als team verantwoordelijk te zijn - being responsible as a team

Other: Ah... ja... dan zit u hier goed - Oh yes, well, you are at the right place then

You: Dat denk ik ook, ja - I think so, too, yes

From here, the conversation will probably go into more detail. Every job interview is different, but be sure to let the interviewers know when you do not understand their Dutch. There is no shame in indicating your limits. Also, tell them that you are a quick learner and will pick up the necessary words and lingo fast. Here is how you can tell them:

You: Ik kan u niet meer goed volgen, sorry - I'm not following anymore/any longer, sorry

You: Ik volg het Nederlands niet meer, sorry - I cannot understand the Dutch anymore, sorry

Other: Dat is niet erg, we gaan verder in Engels, oké? - That is no problem, we'll continue in English, all right?

You: Heel graag, dank u wel - Oh yes, please, thank you

You: Ik pik dingen snel op – I am a quick learner

You: Ik leer de nodige woorden en vaktermen snel – I learn the necessary words and technical terms quickly!

You: Dat weet ik zeker! – I know for sure!

Buying Things

When in the Netherlands, or someplace else where the people speak Dutch, you will need to go shopping at some point, at least for food. A grocery store would be the easiest option. There, you collect your items and then check out. However, what if you cannot find all the things you need? Who do you ask?

Usually, there are some employees in the store, either stocking shelves or advising customers. Be polite and let them finish any current conversations that are having with another customer. Of course, when employees are talking amongst each other, you may interrupt...

You: Hallo, waar kan ik de melk vinden? – Hello, where can I find the milk?

Other: Tweede rij, rechts, mevrouw/meneer – Second row to the right, ma'am/sir

You: Oké, dank je wel! – Okay, thanks!

Waar vind ik: – Where do I find:

het bier – beer

de boter – butter

het brood – bread

het broodbeleg – sandwich fillings

de eieren – eggs

de frisdrank – soda drinks

het fruit – fruits

de groenten – vegetables

ingeblikte vis – canned fish

de jam – jam

de kaas – cheese

de koffie – coffee

de kruiden – herbs

het meel – flour

de melk – milk

de ontbijtgranen – breakfast cereals

de pasta – pasta

de peper – pepper

de pindakaas – peanut butter

de shampoo – shampoo

de schoonmaakmiddelen – cleaning products

de thee – tea

het toiletpapier – toilet paper

de verse vis – fresh fish

het vlees – meat

de vleeswaren – cold cuts

het wasmiddel – laundry detergent

de wijn – wine

de yoghurt – yoghurt

de zeep – soap

het zout – salt

When you have found all these items and paid for them, you will probably survive until your next shopping experience. You might also go to a specialized shop, like a butcher, bakery, greengrocer, etc. Then, you must know a thing or two about weight and pieces.

English weights are different from Dutch weights. The Dutch have a kilo (1,000 grams), a pond (half a kilo = 500 grams), and an ons (100 grams)

Roughly, 1 ons (100 grams) = 3.5 ounces; 1 kilo = 35 ounces.

De slager – the butcher

Mag ik van u: – May I have:

Twee ons biefstuk – Seven ounces of steak

Een pond rundvlees – Half a kilo of beef

Een kilo spare ribs – A kilo of pork spare ribs

Drie ons half-om-half gehakt – Ten and a half ounces of mixed minced meat

Betalen: – to pay:

You: Hoeveel krijgt u van me? – How much will that be?

Other: twintig euro dertig (€20.30) – Twenty euros and thirty cents

You: kan ik pinnen? – Can I use my bank/debit card?

Other: jazeker, maar geen creditcard – Yes, sure, but no credit cards

You: kan ik cash betalen? – Can I pay cash?

Other: natuurlijk – Sure

You: kunt u vijftig euro wisselen? – Do you have change for a fifty?

Other: nee, helaas niet =–No, I am afraid not

You: oh, dan moet ik toch pinnen – Oh, then I need to use my bank/debit card

In the Netherlands, the currency is the euro, just like in the rest of the EU (European Union). This is the symbol of the euro: €. Dutch uses the metrical system, so 1 euro has 100 cents.

The banknotes are €5.00, €10.00, €20.00, €50.00, €100.00, €200.00, and €500.00.

NOTE: No shop will accept banknotes larger than €100.00, as they are afraid of counterfeit money. Even a €100,00 note is viewed suspiciously. So, if you change money before entering the Netherlands (or any other country of the EU), make sure you only get the smaller banknotes.

The euro has coins of €2.00, €1.00, €0.50, €0.20, €0.10, €0.05, €0.02, and €0.01. Although they are official coins, the Netherlands does not use the 1 and 2 cents anymore. The total amount you pay in a shop or market is rounded up or down to 5 cents. Here, sometimes you win, sometimes you lose... In the end, it all evens out!

However, in many other European countries, where the euro is used, the two smallest coins are still in circulation. So they might end up in your wallet anyway—you just cannot spend them in all countries.

De bakker – the bakery

het brood – brood

het broodje – roll

de croissant – croissant

een half bruin brood – half a loaf of brown bread

een heel bruin brood – a loaf of brown bread

een heel volkorenbrood – a loaf of whole wheat bread

het harde broodje – hard roll

de krentenbol – a currant bun

een wit brood – a loaf of white bread

De groenteman – the greengrocer

de aardbei – strawberry

de andijvie – endives

de appel – apple

de banaan – banana

de bloemkool – cauliflower

de boerenkool – kale

de broccoli – broccoli

de champignon – mushroom

de druif – grape

het erwtje – pea

het fruit – fruits (singular in Dutch)

de kers – cherry

de kiwi – kiwi

de knoflook – garlic

de kool – cabbage

de mandarijn – tangerine/mandarin

de peer – pear

de pruim – prune

de sinaasappel – orange

sla – lettuce

spinazie – spinach

de ui – onion

de wortel – carrot

de zuurkool – sauerkraut

Tiny task #10:

Try to come up with ten small conversations in Dutch involving bread, meat, vegetables, and fruits. Ask for the items, the price, and order a certain amount. Write them down and repeat them out loud several times, to get used to these everyday things. You will need them daily. So, start chewing on them...

Greetings

If you are continuously frequenting places, such as apartment buildings, offices, workshops, or building sites, you will naturally get to know some people. Therefore, you need to greet them before striking up a conversation.

Hé, hallo – Hey, hello

Hallo, hoe is het? – Hello, how are you?

Hallo, alles goed? – Hello, you're okay?

Hé, lang niet gezien – Hey, long time no see

Ja joh, hoe is het met je? – Yeah, man, how are you?

Goed wel, en met jou? – Just fine, you?

Met mij gaat het goed – I am fine

Lekker weer, hè? – Nice weather, huh?

Wat een rotweer – Such lousy weather

Ik haat die regenbuien – I hate rainstorms

Ik heb een hekel aan harde wind – I really dislike a hard/severe wind

Tot ziens – See you later

Tot morgen = Until/see you tomorrow

Ik zie jullie morgen – See you guys tomorrow!

Tot zaterdag – See you Saturday

Tot volgende week – See you next week

Dàag! (or: dag) – Bye

Doei (more popular) – Bye

Fijne avond – Enjoy your evening

Fijn weekend = Enjoy your weekend

Veel plezier straks! – Have fun (later on)

Welterusten - Good night

Slaap lekker - Sleep well

Hé, ik heb je gemist! - Hey, I have missed you!

Waar was je? - Where were you?

Ik was ziek - I was ill/sick

Ik was met vakantie - I was on vacation

Ik had een cursus - I was taking a course

Goed dat je er weer bent! - Nice to have you back again

Het is fijn om weer terug te zijn - It is nice to be back

Ik had wel langer willen wegblijven - I could have stayed away longer

More formal:

Goedemorgen - Good morning

Goedemiddag - Good afternoon

Goedenavond - Good evening

Goedemorgen allemaal - Good morning all!

Fijn u te zien - Good to see you

Tot ziens - Goodbye

In general, Dutch people are not that formal. Yet they do not want you to get the impression that they don't care about formality. They do. However, as soon as formalities are over and done with, they shift into a more laidback way of dealing with each other.

The big question is: When are the formalities over? Well, that is hard to say. It all depends on the situation. Sometimes, formalities are never over. For example, when you deal with people much older than you, or "higher" in society than you.

There are people you meet who you pay respect to by being polite. Think of the people who keep society going: community workers, medical workers, social workers, garbage workers, (street)cleaners, firefighters, police, housekeeping in hotels, and so on.

Out of respect for what they do, you could politely approach them. People who are not that high on the social ladder because of their profession or job will appreciate your politeness. After all, you do not know them, and they don't know you... but they provide you with a service you should be grateful for.

Back to the informal Dutch way... Once you are familiar with your coworkers, you will call them by their first name. You will say "jij" instead of "u." This might happen on day one, or in week two, depending on the culture of the company or institution you are working for. Sometimes the head of the department is always addressed as "meneer," "mevrouw," and "u." The same might go for the *big boss*, the owner of the company. However, firms and companies usually have a more informal approach, which does not suggest any lack of respect. Informal does not equal (≠) a lack of respect!

Asking Questions

In this section, you won't find answers to the most important questions in your life; however, it will help you formulate them and other questions in Dutch.

Here are some interrogative pronouns. That is how you form a question, to which you hope to get an answer:

hoe – how

waar – where

waarom – why

wanneer – when

wat – what

welk(e) – what/which

wie – who

It does not matter whether the question implies a person or an object, and even the adverbs "wanneer" and "hoe" can be used freely. They remain adverbs but don't worry about that here.

Unlike the English language, Dutch does not have an auxiliary verb in some questions, like "to do." For instance:

Wie is die man? – Who is that man?

Wie gaat er mee vanavond? – Who is coming along, tonight?

Wie heeft mijn zoon gezien? – Who has seen my son?

Wie komt daar binnen? – Who is coming in?

> Wat eten jullie vanavond? – What do you eat/are you eating tonight?

> Wat heb jij gisteren gezien? – What did you see yesterday?

> Wat hoor ik? – What do I hear?

> Wat hebben jullie besproken? – What did you talk about?

Welk boek vind jij mooier? – Which book do you like best?*

Welke kleur heeft jouw auto? – What color is your car?

Welk shirt staat mij beter? – Which shirt looks best on me?

Van welke muziek houd jij? – What music do you like/love?

*When "what" is used in a very general sense, it is the equivalent of the English "what." If there is a choice involved, the English use "which." The Dutch do not make that distinction.

Waar gaan zij naar toe? – Where do they go (to)?

Waar heb jij mijn kleren gelegd? – Where did you put my clothes?

Waar vind ik hier nog wilde bloemen? – Where do I find wildflowers here?

Waar gaat de reis naar toe? – Where does the trip take you/us/him

Waarom zijn wij hier en nu? – Why are we here and now?

Waarom houdt hij niet van mij? – Why doesn't he love me?

Waarom is de trein zo laat? – Why is the train late?

Waarom weten wij van niets? – Why don't we know anything?

Wanneer komen jullie hier? – When will you come over?

Vertel me wanneer ik klaar moet zijn – Tell me when I have to be ready

Wanneer vertel je me de waarheid? – When are you going to tell me the truth?

Wanneer komen de kinderen thuis? – When will the children be/come home?

Hoe heeft dit kunnen gebeuren? – How could this happen/have happened?

Hoe moet ik u nu noemen? – How should I call you, then?

Hoe werkt dit computerprogramma? – How does this computer program work?

Hoe red ik me uit deze situatie? – How do I get out of/escape from this situation?

Tiny task #11:

Questions, questions, questions... Now, you can ask several of them, using the interrogative pronouns you just learned. And while you are at it, how about forming an answer to them as well?

Example:

– Hoe werkt dit keukenapparaat? Dat kun je beter aan mijn vader vragen.

– Hoe laat vertrekt de trein naar Amsterdam? De volgende trein vertrekt om kwart over vier.

Not that hard, huh? Write down ten of these sets and call yourself an advanced speaker of Dutch!

Buying and Ordering

People buy a lot during their lives. They consume and consume; sometimes, they like to, need to, or just cannot resist.

Many of these things can now be purchased online, and usually, Dutch websites also have an English version—or they are so straightforward that you can navigate them without much difficulty. In this section, though, you will only learn how to buy items from physical stores, and later, how to order at a restaurant.

In many shops, you can browse without a shop attendant at your side. If an attendant does approach you when you enter, you can simply make it clear that you would like to look around by yourself.

You walk in...

> Attendant: Goedemiddag, kan ik u helpen? – Good afternoon, may I help you?

> You: Ik wil graag even rondkijken – I would like to have a look around

> Att: Natuurlijk, gaat uw gang – Of course, please do

> You: Dank u wel – Thank you

> Att: Kunt u het vinden? – Can you find what you are looking for?

> Att: Wat zoekt u precies? – What exactly are you looking for?

You: Hmm... moeilijk te zeggen – Hmm... hard to say

You: Hmn... weet nog niet – Hmm... don't know yet...

You: Ik kijk nog even verder... – I will continue browsing...

If you need assistance due to not knowing quite what you want, this is the moment to ask for it.

You: Ik zoek een overhemd – I am looking for a shirt,

You: Niet te formeel, niet te casual – Not too formal, not too casual

You: Iets er tussenin, eigenlijk... – Something in between, really...

Att: Aan welke kleur denkt u? – What color should that be?

You: Geen idee – No idea

Att: Wat is uw boordmaat? – What is the size of your collar?

You: Um... 43, geloof ik – Um... 43, I think

Att: Ik meet het even op... – I will take your measurement

You: Oké... – Okay...

After the attendant gets you the right item, if you do not like it:

You: Ik vind dit niet echt mooi – I really don't like this

You: Er zit niet echt iets tussen – There is nothing you showed me I really like

You: Misschien moet ik even verder kijken – Maybe I should look someplace else

You: Ik denk dat ik even verder kijk – I think I'll look elsewhere

You: Dank u wel voor de moeite – Thank you for your assistance

You: Dank u wel voor uw hulp – Thank you for your help

There are hundreds of things to shop for in a shopping area. Sometimes you might walk around such a place, with your partner, friend, or child, without really having something in mind to purchase. Just browsing is fun! In Dutch, you call that: Winkelen – shopping.

"Winkelen" is spending time in a shopping mall or shopping area without a plan. The chances are that you go home with nothing, or go home with a few items you may or may not need... Arriving home with several bags could be the moment you regret spending all that money...

If that is the case, you should not open or use whatever you don't need or want. Leave the tag on, don't remove it from its packaging, and return it to the shop as soon as possible with the receipt. You have a right to return purchased items within fifteen or 30 days from the day they were purchased. However, the condition of the item(s) must be unused or uneaten for food products.

Some shops will give you your money back; however, most shops will offer a voucher to redeem in the store. Beware, though, as most vouchers have an expiration date.

You: Ik kom dit terugbrengen – I would like to return this item

You: Het past niet goed – It doesn't fit well*

You: De kleur is niet goed – The color isn't right*

You: Mijn man/vrouw vindt het niet mooi – My husband/wife doesn't like it*

Att: Wil u iets anders uitzoeken? – Do you want to exchange it for something else?

You: Nee, niet nu. Ik wil mijn geld terug – No, not now. I would like my money back, please

Att: Sorry, wij geven geen geld terug – Sorry, we don't give refunds

Att: Ik kan u een waardebon geven – I can give you a voucher

Att: Die kunt u bij uw volgende aankoop gebruiken – You can use it with your next purchase

You: Kunt u echt geen geld teruggeven? – You really cannot give me my money back?

You: Ik kom hier niet vaak. Ik woon in xxxx – I don't come here often. I live in xxxx

Att: Het spijt me, dat gaat echt niet. – I am sorry, that is not an option

You: Nou, wel vervelend... – Oh, that's a bummer...

*NOTE: In most cases, you do not have to explain why you are returning an item to the shop. However, REMEMBER to keep the

receipt and return the item within the exchange or refund purchasing window; otherwise, the retailer can refuse to take it back. If you don't have the time to return a purchase, call the shop and inform them. Tell them when you can return it. If the employee or manager agrees, ask for their name so that you have a reference when you return to the shop.

Vocabulary - Clothing

de bh – bra

de bikini – bikini

de blouse – blouse

de broek – pair of trousers

de hoge hak(ken) – high heel(s)

het jasje – jacket

de jeans/spijkerbroek – jeans

de jurk – dress

de korte broek – shorts

de korte mouw – short sleeve

de laars/laarzen – boot(s)

de lange mouw – long sleeve

de legging – leggings

de onderbroek – briefs/boxers

het ondergoed – underwear

het overhemd – shirt

het shirt – shirt

de rok – skirt

de schoen(en) – shoe(s)

het slipje – knickers/undies/panties

de sok(ken) – sock(s)

de stropdas – tie

de sweater – sweater

de top – top

de trui – sweater/pullover/jumper

het t-shirt – T-shirt

zonder mouwen – sleeveless

de zwembroek – swimsuit/swimming trunks

Vocabulary – Miscellaneous Items

het accessoire – accessory

het boek/de boeken – book/books

de broodrooster – toaster

de droger – dryer

de drogisterij – drugstore

het eetcafé – bistro/diner

de elektronica – electronics

de handtas – bag/ladies bag

het huishoudtextiel – linens

het keukenapparaat – kitchen appliance

de keukenspullen – kitchen equipment/tools

de koffiebar – coffee corner

de spullen – stuff/things

de lederwaren – leather goods

de parfumerie – perfumery

de wasmachine – washing machine

de waterkoker – electric kettle

Taking a cab...

Tired from shopping? Want to get home or to your hotel or apartment to take a well-deserved rest? Well, in the Netherlands, you cannot hail a cab (in Dutch, a "taxi"). Instead, you must walk to the nearest taxi stand/rank and select the first taxi in the line, or wait in a queue. Make sure the taxi driver puts the meter on (the starting rate is relatively high, compared to other countries).

There is Uber, but at the current time (spring, 2020), the Uber grid is not that well established, except for the bigger cities like Amsterdam. It is possible to get a driver from several miles away, but be aware that the cost will go up significantly since the driver needs to cover his/her costs.

At Schiphol Airport and some of the bigger train stations in the country, non-licensed taxi drivers try to hustle rides. While this is understandable—everyone needs to make a living—these so-called "snorders" (crawlers) are disliked by taxi drivers who have an expensive *license* to renew every year. If you select a "snorder," you might end up in a confrontation between them and the taxi drivers.

Entering a restaurant...

Staff: Goedenavond mevrouw, meneer – Good evening, madame, sir

You: Goedenavond, heeft u plaats voor twee? – Good evening, do you have a table for two?

Staff: Hebtt u gereserveerd? – Do you have a reservation?

You: Nee, we hebben niet gereserveerd – No, we don't have a reservation

Staff: Eens kijken... ik heb hier nog een tafeltje – Let me see... I have a table over here

You: Fijn, dank u wel – Great. Thank you

You: Hebtt u geen tafel bij het raam? – Don't you have a table near the window?

You: Mogen we iets rustiger zitten? – May we have a quieter place?

Staff: Natuurlijk. Komt u maar mee – Of course. Come with me, please

Staff: Helaas, dit is nog de enige tafel – Sorry, this is the only table left

You: Wij hebben gereserveerd – We have a reservation

You: Onder de naam xxxx – The name is xxxx

You: Wij zijn met één persoon meer/minder – We are with one person less/more

Staff: Oh, dat hindert niet – Oh, no problem

You: Fijn – Good

Staff: Wil u alvast iets drinken? – Can I get you something to drink?

Staff: Kan ik iets voor u inschenken? – May I pour you a drink?

You: We wachten even tot we bestellen – We will wait until we order

You: Ja graag.... Doet u maar een pilsje – Yes, please.... I will have a beer

You: En een... droge witte wijn – And a... dry white wine

Staff: Komt er aan – Coming right up

Staff: De menukaarten, en de wijnkaart – The menus, and the wine list

Staff: De weekspecialiteiten staan op het bord – This week's specialties are on the board

While you sip your aperitif, you might browse the menu, the board on the wall, and check the wine list. You can also decide to have something else to drink. However, just tap water is not enough. Restaurants expect you to order something from the bar, whether alcoholic or non-alcoholic. If you want wine, you can order it by the glass or bottle, with some wines only by the bottle, as indicated on the wine list.

If you order a bottle of wine, you will usually first be asked to taste it—unless you are in a simple bistro with a choice of only two or three wines. In this case, the bottle will just be placed on the table.

When wine tasting...

Staff: wie gaat de wijn proeven? – Who is going to taste the wine?

You: Ik/mijn vrouw/vriend/man doe(t) dat – I/my wife/friend/husband will

> You: Mmm... lekker. Prima. U kunt inschenken – Mmm good. Fine. You can pour the wine
>
> You: Hmm... uh... hij is een beetje wrang – Hmm... uh... it is a bit sour
>
> Staff: Echt waar? Ik haal een andere fles – Really? I'll get you another bottle
>
> Staff: Het is een erg droge wijn – It is a very dry wine
>
> Staff: U raakt zo aan de smaak gewend – You will acquire the taste real fast
>
> You: De wijn heeft kurk – The wine is corked
>
> You: De wijn is te warm – The wine is too warm
>
> You: Hmm... ik vind hem niet lekker – Hmm... I don't really like it

NOTE: In a bistro, the wine can easily have too high a temperature as there is no wine fridge. You are not supposed to fuss over the wine temperature, though. Corked wine is another thing, of course. The glass in which the wine is served might be basic as well.

However, when the wine's price is over 25 euros a bottle, expect an appropriate glass and temperature. In high-end restaurants, you do not refill your glass; the waiter does. So, sit back and enjoy it!

Most Dutch restaurants, even the small bistros, have an English version of the menu, or an English translation under the various dishes or courses. Here are some main terms:

Vocabulary - Restaurant Food

de aardappelpuree – mashed potatoes

het appeldessert – apple dessert

de appeltaart – apple pie

de biefstuk – steak

de crème brulée – crème brûlée

doorbakken – well done (i.e., for a cooked steak)

de eend – duck

frietjes – chips/French fries

het gevogelte – fowl

het filet – fillet

de groenten van het seizoen – seasonal vegetables

het hoofdgerecht – main course

de maaltijd – meal

het kaasplankje – cheese plate

het kalfsvlees – veal

het kalfs/varkensmedaillon – medallion of veal/pork

de kip – chicken

de lamsbout – leg of lamb

het lamskarbonaadje – lamb chop

het lamsvlees – lamb

medium gebakken – medium done (i.e., for a cooked steak)

roze – pink

het nagerecht/toetje – dessert/sweet

de salade – salad

de soep – soup

de soep van de dag – soup of the day

de varkenshaas – pork tenderloin

de varkenskarbonade – pork chop

het varkensvlees – pork

het visgerecht – fish course

de visgraat – fish bone

het voorgerecht – appetizer

het ijs – ice cream

Smakelijk eten! – Enjoy your meal!

Alles naar wens? – Everything fine?

Bent u klaar? – Are you done?

Was alles naar wens? – Was everything fine?

And how does your meal taste?

Mmm... lekker – Mmm... good

Wow, dit is lekker! – Wow, this is delicious!

Proef eens – Here, have a taste

Mag ik eens proeven? – Can I taste it?

Hmm... wel een beetje zout – Hmm... a bit salty to my taste

Er zit veel peper in, lekker! – It has a lot of pepper, yummy!

Jakkie... knoflook, dat lust ik niet – Ew... garlic, I don't like garlic

Woohoo, dit is echt heerlijk – Woohoo... this is really delicious!

De soep is koud... bah – The soup is cold... yuck/ugh

Ik vind dit niet lekker ruiken – I don't think it smells nice

Er moeten meer kruiden in – It needs more herbs

Jij weet niet wat lekker is – You don't know what's good

Ik houd niet van vet aan het vlees – I don't like fat on my meat

After you finish your meal:

Wil u de kaart nog zien? – Would you like to see the menu again?

Voor het dessert? – For dessert?

Wil u de dessertkaart? – Would you like the dessert menu?

Koffie? – Would you like some coffee?

Mag ik de rekening? – May I have the check/bill, please

Ik wil graag contant betalen – I would like to pay in cash

Ik wil graag pinnen – I would like to use a card, please

As for tipping the staff... Dutch staff members of restaurants, cafés, and the like are paid according to a collective labor agreement, just as most employees in the Netherlands. There is no percentage of the service charge added to the restaurant check. Yet their wages are not very high, either. Many staff members work at minimum wage but provide excellent service. So, if you are happy with their service, leave a few euros for the so-called "fooienpot" (tip jar). Whether there is a jar or the staff member may keep the tip for him/herself, is not your concern... So, the happier you are, the more you tip. Also, if the amount you must pay is over 100 euros and you leave them 50 cents, that is considered an insult. Tip at least five percent.

Vocabulary – Eating Out

alvast – in the meantime/already/meanwhile

bah – yuck/ugh

het bier – beer

het bord – the board (on the wall)

het bord – the plate (on the table)

contant (betalen) – (to pay) cash

de dessertkaart – dessert menu

droog/droge – dry

de fles – bottle

de flessenopener – bottle opener

heerlijk – delicious

hinderen – to be a problem

inschenken – to pour

heeft kurk – is corked (wine)

de knoflook – garlic

kruiden – herbs

kurk – cork

lekker – nice/delicious

meer – more

de menukaart – menu

minder – less

de opener – bottle opener

het pilsje/biertje – beer (from the tap)

de peper – pepper

pinnen – to charge/to use a card

proeven – to taste

het raam – window

de rekening – bill/check

ruiken – to smell

reserveren – to reserve/to book

de reservering – reservation

rustig – quiet

de specerij – spice/condiment

de specialiteit – specialty

de tafel – table

het tafeltje – small table

te warm – too warm (wine)

te – too

het vet – fat

de weekspecialiteit(en) – weekly specialty/specialties

wennen aan – to acquire

de wijnkaart – wine list

witte wijn – white wine

wrang – sour

zó (= snel) – (real) fast

het zout – salt

At Work

At your workplace, you need to be able to greet, converse, or generally chat with your employer, colleagues, and clients. Thus, it is time to get sociable, work together, and have a meeting...

Goedemorgen/middag/avond, allemaal! – Good morning/afternoon/evening, everybody!

Ik ga koffie halen. Wil iemand iets? – I am going to the coffee machine. Anybody?

Hé, ga je naar de koffieautomaat? – Hey, are you going to the coffee machine?

Wil je voor mij een dubbele espresso meenemen? – Could you bring me a double espresso, please?

Dank je wel. Je bent geweldig... – Thanks. You are great...

Ga je naar de voorraadkamer? – Are you going to the supply room?

Ik moet ook die kant op. – I have to go there, too

Zal ik met je meelopen? – Mind if I join you?

Kun je voor mij printpapier meenemen? – Can you bring me paper for the printer?

Ja zeg, ik ben je knechtje niet... – Come on, I am not your servant...

Natuurlijk, net zo makkelijk – Of course, no problem

Wie weet hoe de printer werkt? – Does anyone know how the printer works?

De inkt is op! – The ink ran out!

De kopieermachine loopt vast. Help! – Oh help! The copying machine got jammed!

Houd eens op met dat gezeur – Stop whining, please

Het is altijd hetzelfde met jou – It is always the same story with you

We hebben het allemaal druk, hoor – We are all busy here, though

Jij bent niet de enige – You are not the only one

Als je problemen hebt, ga je naar de teamleider – If you have problems, you go to the team leader

Laat ons gewoon ons werk doen, alsjeblieft – Please, let us do our job, okay?

Ga je mee lunchen? – Are you coming for lunch?

Even dit afmaken, ik kom zo – I want to finish this. I'll be there shortly

Nee, ik lunch buiten de deur – No, I am having lunch someplace else

Aha... leuke afspraak? – Aha... a date, maybe?

Huh, bemoei je er niet mee... – Mind your own business, huh...

Ja...! Ik weet het zeker – Yes!... I am sure of it!

Joh, houd op, nou... - Get out of here...!

Ik lunch met iemand van de voetbalclub - I am having lunch with someone from the soccer club

Moeten we dat geloven? - You want us to believe that?

Ja, doei! - Yeah, right...

Hoi, kun je me even helpen? - Hi, can you give me a hand, please?

Ik loop vast op dit probleem - I am stuck on this problem

Ik weet niet hoe ik dit moet oplossen - I have no clue how to solve this

Ik heb al van alles geprobeerd - I have tried several options already

En er is haast bij deze klus - And this job is an urgent one

Er is geen haast bij, hoor - There is no rush

Kan het wachten? - Can it wait?

Wacht even, ik kom zo - Hold on, I'll be right with you

Dat kun je beter aan xxx vragen - You'd better ask xxx

Hallo, klantenservice - Hello, customer service

U spreekt met xxx - My name is xxx

Waar kan ik u mee helpen? - How may I assist you?

Wat is het bestelnummer? - What is the order number?

Wat is het referentienummer? - What is the reference number?

Wat is uw BSN? - What is your social security number? BSN = Burger Service Nummer

Wat is uw polisnummer? - What is your policy number?

Een ogenblik, alstublieft - Hold on, please

Ik moet u doorverwijzen naar - I must refer you to

Een andere afdeling/systeembeheer – Another department/system management

Er zijn nog acht wachtenden vóór u – There are eight people waiting

Bedankt voor het wachten – Thank you for waiting

Wil jij met mij een dienst ruilen? – Are you willing to swap a shift with me?

Ja hoor, om welke dag gaat het? – Sure, what day are we talking about?

Oh, je wil een avond kwijt? – Oh, you want to get rid of an evening?

Balen... maar goed, ik heb ja gezegd – Bummer... but fine, I agreed to swap...

Volgende keer kom ik bij jou! – You owe me one!

Nee, ik wil niet ruilen – No, I don't want to swap.

Ik heb nou net eens een fijn rooster – I happen to have a roster that suits me well...

Je wil altijd ruilen met me – You always want to swap with me

Probeer maar eens iemand anders – Try someone else, for a change

Vocabulary – At Work

de afdeling – department

afmaken – to finish

balen – bummer

bemoeien – to mind one's business

het BSN – social security number

de bestelling – order

de dienst – shift

doorverwijzen – to refer

druk zijn – being busy

geloven – to believe

zeuren – to whine

helpen – to assist/to help

iemand – anyone/someone

ja, doei – yeah, right...

die kant op moeten – to have to go there

de klantenservice – customer service

het knechtje – servant

koffie halen – to get some coffee

de koffiemachine – coffee machine

de kopie – copy

de kopieermachine – the copying machine

kwijt raken/kwijt willen – to lose/to get rid of

meegaan – to come for

meelopen (letterlijk) – to walk along (literally)

meelopen/meeloper (figuurlijk) – to follow/the follower (metaphorically)

meenemen – to take/bring/get me

het nummer – number

het ogenblik – hold on

ophouden! (vrolijk) – get out of here (friendly, jokingly)

ophouden (serieus) – to stop (seriously)

op zijn – to run out

de polis – policy

proberen – to try

de referentie – reference

het rooster – roster

ruilen – to swap

het systeembeheer – system management

de voorraadkamer – supply room

wachten – waiting

wachtenden vóór u – x number of people waiting

werken (arbeid) – to work (as in a job)

werken (functioneren) – to function

zeker – sure

At School/College

If you are trying to better your position at work by completing a course, or are spending a year in the Netherlands for education, you will mingle with classmates, teachers, professors, and tutors. So, here are some phrases that will help you as you learn:

You: Goedemorgen, ik zoek lokaal 12 – Good morning, I am looking for classroom 12

You: Waar kan ik dat vinden – Where do I go?

Other: Je neemt de trap naar de eerste etage, dan ga je linksaf – You take the stairs to the first floor, then you take a left

You: Dank u wel – Thank you

You: Hoi, is dit lokaal 12? – Hi, is this classroom 12?

Other: Ja, klopt. Kom binnen – Yes, it is. Come in

You: Hoi, ik ben Karl – Hi, I'm Karl

Other: Hoi, Karl, ik ben Sophie – Hi, Karl, I am Sophie

Other: En dit is Freddie – And this is Freddie

You: Hallo, Freddie, Sophie – Hello, Freddie, Sophie

You: Zijn jullie hier ook nieuw? – Are you new here as well?

Sophie: Freddie wel, ik heb hier al een cursus gedaan – Freddie is, I already took a course here

You: Vind je het hier leuk? – Do you like it here?

Sophie: Oh ja, dit is een geweldige school – Oh yeah, this is a great college

You: Ik ga hier drie cursussen volgen – I am going to do three courses here

Freddie: Oei! Wat een ijver! Ik maar een – Oh! What diligence! I only do one

Sophie: Daar komt de leraar – The teacher is here

Sophie: Laten we gaan zitten – Let's take a seat

Sophie: Oh, er zijn negen cursisten – Oh, there are nine students

You: Fijn, gelukkig geen grote groep – Good, fortunately not a big group

Freddie: Er zitten hooguit zestien mensen in een groep – There are at most sixteen people in a group

You: Hmm... meer moeten het er niet zijn – Hmm... that's really enough

Sophie: Ach man, wat kan het je schelen? – Come on, who cares anyway?

Sophie: Het meeste doe je toch thuis – Most of the studying you do at home

You: Ik vind het vervelend als mensen maar blijven hangen in vragen – I don't like it when people keep asking questions

Freddie: Wie zegt nou dat ze dat doen? – Who knows if they'll do that?

You: Nou, met een grotere groep is die kans ook groter – Well, in a bigger group, chances are bigger as well

Freddie: Kom op, we zijn hier om te leren – Oh well, we are here to learn, aren't we?

Teacher: Dames, heren, ik ben Theo – Ladies, gentlemen, my name is Theo

Teacher: Ik ben jullie leraar de komende twaalf weken – I am your teacher for the next twelve weeks

Teacher: Ik begin telkens strikt op tijd – I start strictly on time, every time

Teacher: Dus kom op tijd – So, be on time, please

Teacher: Halverwege pauzeren we twintig minuten – There's a twenty-minute break halfway

Teacher: Anders houd je geen drie uur vol – Otherwise you won't last three hours.

Teacher: We gaan beginnen! – Let's start!

Vocabulary – School/College

anders – otherwise/different (noun)

de cursist – student

de cursus – course/class

de etage – floor

gaan zitten – to take a seat

de groep – group

halverwege – halfway

hooguit – at most

de leraar – teacher (male or female)

de lerares – teacher (female)

leren – to learn

leuk vinden – to like

linksaf – to take a left

het (klas)lokaal – classroom

nieuw – new

op tijd komen – to be on time

pauzeren – to take a break

schelen – to care

de school – school/college

strikt – strict(ly)

volhouden/uithouden – to last

de vraag – the question

wat kan het je schelen – who cares

de trap – stairs

de ijver – diligence

ijverig – diligent

There you go! Your first course has just started. Of course, it will be hard to be follow a course in the Dutch language. But what a challenge! Make that brain of yours work!

Once you get settled in, things will be easier. Remember: Always ask people around you if you get stuck because of the language barrier. Although you have come a long way, practice makes perfect.

Take a look at another situation...

You: Dat was niet zo heel moeilijk – That wasn't too hard

You: Maar ik heb wel nieuwe dingen geleerd – But I did learn some new things

Other: Ik vond het best moeilijk, hoor – Well, I thought it was pretty hard

Other: Allemaal nieuw voor mij – Everything was new for me

You: Heb je alles begrepen? – Did you understand all of it?

You: Als je wil, help ik je wel – If you want, I can help you

You: Dan leg ik je uit wat je niet snapt – I can explain what you don't get

Other: Dank je! Dat is heel aardig van je – Thanks, that is really nice of you

You: Geen probleem, ik doe het graag – No problem, I will be glad to

The best way to get acquainted with some of your fellow students is to help someone with something they do not understand or vice versa.

You: Poeh, dat was pittig vandaag – Ouch, that was kind of tough today

You: Ik kon de helft niet volgen – I couldn't follow half of it

You: En ik kon geen vraag stellen – And I couldn't ask one single question

You: Iedereen had zo veel vragen – Everybody had so many questions

Other: Ik kan je wel wat uitleggen, als je wil – I can explain a few things, if you'd like me to

You: Zou je dat willen doen? Geweldig! – Would you really do that? Fantastic!

You: Wanneer heb je tijd? – When will it suit you?

Other: Vanmiddag kan wel – I can do it this afternoon

Other: Dan kun je goed verder leren – Then studying will be a lot easier

You: Dat is echt te gek! Heel erg fijn! – That's really awesome! Great!

All this helping is a perfect way to get to know each other. After the serious business, you can get a coffee together, for instance. The next time you see each other, you can also chat much easier.

Another way to get acquainted with a fellow student is to suggest studying together, be it in the library or at somebody's home. Dutch students are very sociable and willing to help someone in the early stage of their learning. And, of course, you yourself can figure out some ways to connect with other students. Remember: It is always a bit harder for the solo person to mingle with others. It really takes some effort, especially when you notice people have already befriended each other. Then it is harder to get included in the already established group. That does not mean you have to become "chummy" with the "goofball" of the group. Just tread carefully, and don't lose patience too soon. You will get there.

Any Questions?

You will likely have questions for your teacher or professor during class. It is simple: when you have questions, you ask them. But at the right time. This is important. You cannot interrupt a lecture in an auditorium. At the end of the lecture, usually, there will be an opportunity to ask questions. So, write your question(s) down and fire away when the time is right.

When the course or class is less formal, there is typically enough room to ask the teacher questions. It is important here, too, not to interrupt while the teacher is speaking about the subject. Wait for a break in his/her teaching, then ask. Interrupting while someone else is speaking is not polite, and certainly not in situations where you are more or less dependent on someone (i.e., a teacher, professor, etc.).

Another thing to remember is the difference between asking a question and initiating a discussion. Of course, you know that difference! However, sometimes one forgets in the heat of the moment. When something is unclear to you, you can ask about it—at the appropriate moment. You ask, and hopefully, the teacher will explain it to you.

Sometimes there is a discussion on a certain matter in class. Through discussion, you can learn a lot—if you are open-minded enough. Here you can also discuss the point of view of the teacher/professor... after all, it is a discussion time! Only narrow-minded teachers will not be amused when their point of view is "criticized." It is up to you to judge if your teacher is one of them.

Whenever you criticize someone's point of view or opinion, whether it is a student's or a teacher's, always be kind and civil. The old saying: "treat everyone the way you would like to be treated yourself" is certainly applicable here!

You: Mevrouw, meneer, ik begrijp iets niet - Excuse me, madam, sir, there is something I don't understand

Teacher: En wat is dat? - What is it?

You: Karl, ik heet Karl - Karl, my name is Karl

Teach: Oké, Karl, wat begrijp je niet? - Okay, Karl, what is it you don't understand?

You: U had het over xxxx, maar ik snap niet hoe u daartoe komt. - You mentioned xxxx, but I don't understand how you got to that?

You: De formule/benadering, bedoel ik - The formula/approach, I mean

Teach: Ah, ik begrijp het. Laat me het nog een keer uitleggen - Ah, I see. Let me explain it to you again

Teach: Zijn er anderen die het ook niet begrijpen, misschien? - Is there anyone else who doesn't understand this?

Teach: Kijk eens aan, je bent niet de enige, Karl - Well, well, you are not the only one, Karl

Teach: Goed, nog een keer... - Okay, here we go again...

NOTE: It is always better to mention your name first if the group exceeds eight students... That makes it easier for the teacher!

After the explanation, you hopefully understand. If not, let the teacher know, but specify what you do not get exactly. A response like, "I still don't get it" isn't helpful... Stipulate and make it simpler for your teacher to help you understand everything.

When all the explaining is over:

You: Dank u wel, het is me nu duidelijker – Thank you, I understand it better now

You: Dank u wel, ik snap het nu – Thank you, I get it now

You might also need to approach the teacher/professor after class to ask or tell them something. Depending on time, all questions should be short and answered in a minute. Such as:

You: Ik ben er vrijdag helaas niet – I will not be here on Friday

You: Ik moet naar de dokter – I must see my doctor

You: Ik moet voor een onderzoek naar het ziekenhuis – I have to go to the hospital for some tests

You: Ik heb privé-omstandigheden waardoor ik niet kan komen – I have private business to attend

You: Wanneer moeten we de planning voor de scriptie inleveren? – When must we hand in our planning for the thesis?

Teach: Vóór het eind van de maand – Before the end of the month

Teach: Uiterlijk 5 april – April 5 at the latest

You: Mag ik een week uitstel voor xxx – Can I get a week's extension for xxxx

Teach: En waarom dan wel? – And why is that?

You: Ik loop met alles wat achter – I am behind schedule with everything

Teach: Hoe komt dat? – How come?

You: Het gaat niet zo goed allemaal – Things aren't going that well

Teach: Heb je problemen? – Are there any problems?

You: Nee, nee, ik vind het alleen erg moeilijk allemaal, in een vreemde taal – No, no, it is just kind of hard for me in a foreign language

Teach: Ik begrijp het. Je bent toch ook wel Nederlands aan het leren? – I see. You are studying Dutch as well, aren't you?

You: ja, ja, dat doe ik inderdaad. Dat is extra werk boven op de rest – Yes, I do indeed. That is extra work added to the rest

You: Het is soms wat veel – It is a lot sometimes

Teach: Ja, dat is logisch. Je moet een goede planning maken, zodat je niet vastloopt op den duur – Yes, that is understandable. You must make a solid planning, so you don't get overwhelmed

Teach: Vooruit, ik geef je tien dagen extra! – Okay then, I'll give you an additional ten days!

Teach: Gebruik ze goed! – Make good use of them!

Teach: En luister goed: als je het niet redt, ga naar je mentor. Die is er niet voor niets... – And listen, if you don't manage, go to your mentor. We have mentors for a reason, you know...

You: Dat doe ik. Dank u wel! – I will do that. Thank you!

Vocabulary – School and Questions?

aardig – nice

achterlopen – to be behind schedule

de benadering/aanpak – approach

best gemakkelijk – pretty easy

best moeilijk – pretty hard

begrijpen – to understand

de formule – formula

inleveren – to hand in

leren – to learn

moeilijk – hard

de planning – planning

pittig – tough

pittig/e voedsel/kruiden – spicy food/herbs

het probleem – trouble

snappen – to get it

specificeren – to specify

te gek – awesome

uitleggen – to explain

uiterlijk – at the latest

het uitstel – xtension

het uiterlijk – looks

de vraag – question

een vraag stellen – to ask a question

de vreemde taal – foreign language

vreemd – strange, odd

redden – to manage

redden (levens) – to rescue (lives)

As in everyday life, a school, college, university, or an educational institution has social issues and problems. However, you do not have to condone anything that takes place and hurts you in any way—theft, racism, condescending or sexist behavior, abuse, or sexual abuse. No society, however small, is immune to any of these unwanted behaviors.

If this happens to you, make sure you report it to the manager, dean, or a confidential counselor. The latter is best to talk to as they must keep everything confidential. Every college or university has at least one counselor on campus.

You: ik zoek de vertrouwenspersoon – I am looking for the counselor

Counselor: Je hebt hem/haar gevonden! – You found him/her!

You: Hebt u tijd voor mij? – Do you have a moment?

Couns: Natuurlijk, kom binnen – Of course, come in

Couns: Nu niet, over een uur wel - Sorry, not now, in an hour I have time

You: Ik heb een probleem. Ik zit in de problemen - I have a problem. I am in trouble

Couns: Vertel maar, ik luister - Tell me, I am listening

You: Het is nogal um... vervelend - It is kind of um... awkward

Couns: Je kunt hier vrijuit praten - You can talk freely here

You: Ik word lastiggevallen - I am being harassed

You: Ik denk omdat ik anders ben - I think because I am different

Couns: Anders, wat bedoel je? - Different, what do you mean with that?

You: Nou, ik ben... uh... niet hetero - Well, I am... uh... not straight

Couns: Dus je bent homoseksueel - So, you are a homosexual

Couns: Nou en? Dit is de 21e eeuw! - So what? This is the 21st century!

You: Uh... niet iedereen denkt zo - Uh... not everyone thinks that way

Couns: En hoe word je lastiggevallen? - And how are you being harassed?

You: Ze schelden me uit, halen dingen uit mijn tas en gooien die gewoon in het rond - They are calling me names, they take things out of my satchel and throw them around

Couns: Dat is onaanvaardbaar gedrag! - That is unacceptable behavior!

Couns: Wie doet dat? - Who is doing this?

You: Er zijn er drie - There are three of them

You: Maar ik kan u niet zeggen wie - But I cannot give you names

You: Dan wordt het alleen maar erger - Then it will only get worse

You: Maar ik voel me er heel lullig onder - But it makes me feel really bad

Couns: Dat kan ik me voorstellen - I can imagine

Couns: In welke groep gebeurt dit? - In which group does this happen?

You: Europese Studies - In European Studies

Couns: Hmm... oké, als je geen namen wil geven, moeten we het anders aanpakken - Hmm... okay, since you don't want to give me names, we must approach this differently

Couns: Maak je geen zorgen, ik ga er achteraan! - Don't worry, I'm on it!

You: Dank u wel, mevrouw/meneer - Thank you, madame/sir

Vocabulary - Confidential Counselor

aanpakken - to act

aanpakken/aannemen - to accept

aanvaardbaar - acceptable

accepteren, goedkeuren - to condone

(er) achteraan gaan - to be on it

anders - different

de diefstal - theft

de eeuw - century

het gedrag - behavior

hebt u tijd? - do you have a moment?

hetero - straight

de homoseksueel - homosexual

ik voel me lullig* - I really feel bad

lastigvallen - to harass

lullig* – really bad (*"lullig" is a word used in informal conversations only!)

maak je geen zorgen – don't worry

de maatschappelijke problemen – social issues

melden – to report

de mishandeling – abuse

neerbuigend – condescending

onaanvaardbaar – unacceptable

het probleem – trouble/problem

het racisme – racism

rondgooien – to throw around

seksistisch – sexist

seksueel misbruik – sexual abuse

de tas – satchel

uitschelden – to call names

de vertrouwenspersoon – confidential counselor

vervelend – awkward

voorstellen – to imagine

voorstellen (aan iemand) – to introduce (to someone)

voorstellen (een plan) – to propose (a plan, a suggestion)

vrijuit – freely

zich zorgen maken – to worry

de zorg – worry

Of course, these kinds of situations do not only happen at college, university, or other educational institutions. Everywhere in society, narrow-minded people think they can bully others—even in the Netherlands, although known for its laid-back mentality. You can never expect a whole country to be in tune with the correct code of behavior.

It might happen in your job. Any company or firm of any size has a confidential counselor to take care of these kinds of things. If you are working in a small company and there is no such person, talk to your coordinator, or a coworker you trust. Don't bottle it up; speak up. You are within your full rights to do so.

Special Days, Events, and Facts

April 27 is the king's birthday: *Koningsdag* – King's Day. On this day, Koning Willem-Alexander will visit a town or city in the Netherlands. His wife, Queen Maximá, and his three daughters will join him, as will some other members of the royal family. This is quite an honor for the town and a big deal for everybody living there. The entire population of the city or town will assemble in the streets, where all kinds of performances occur. Everyone else can watch the event on television if they are interested.

Also on this day, children sell their toys, books, and knick-knacks on an old sheet or blanket. They claim a spot in a park, on the street, or anywhere these so-called "vrijmarkt" markets are permitted (*vrijmarkt* – garage sale). Along with King's Day, this is also allowed on Liberation Day (*Bevrijdingsdag*) on May 5. It is fun to walk by these places and see the kids doing their best to attract your attention. Kids who play an instrument will also try to collect some euros from passersby.

On both the holidays mentioned above, big outdoor concerts are held on barricaded streets, in a park, or a sports stadium. Many people come out and enjoy themselves. After all, it is the time of year when there is nice weather.

Although the Dutch also have Santa Claus (*de kerstman*), their big December holiday is *Sinterklaas* (Saint Nicholas). This holy bishop came from Turkey originally and then moved to Spain some 1,000 years ago. He is a true friend of small children, bringing them presents from Spain. He arrives in early November on a steamer (*stoomboot*—at least, that's what the kids think; it is just a cargo-vessel) with a bunch of Zwarte Pieten as his assistants. He keeps the kids in suspense for about four weeks, and there is a special candy for this s festivity, which *Zwarte Piet* (Black Pete) throws around. Plus, there are chocolate figurines of Sinterklaas and Zwarte Piet!

Of late, there is a discussion going on as to whether Zwarte Piet is a form of discrimination, and thus not suitable anymore. The national debate was started by some people who felt discriminated against because the Zwarte Pieten resemble slaves. Legend has it that Sinterklaas saved small black kids from slavery in Turkey and took them with him and let them work for a salary. This discussion went international, often out of context. Even the United Nations spoke about it.

As a compromise, some towns/cities now have Pieten in all colors of the rainbow, others keep their Pieten black, and others have white Pieten. If you ever get caught up in this discussion, try to avoid voicing your opinion because you will always offend someone. Those in favor of Zwarte Piet will tell you it is the tradition that counts; those against it will tell you that the stereotypical characteristics of Black Pete are discriminatory. You cannot please everyone, so best to stay out of it.

You might be amazed by the number of bicycles in the Netherlands. There are millions of them. Everybody has at least one bicycle (*de fiets*) or easily two—one for everyday use and one for recreational use. There are many roads/lanes for bicyclists (*het fietspad*), and people are happily using them. People love to ride their bikes for fun as well.

In the cities, do not let the cyclists scare you. They ignore the red traffic light and cross squares and streets as if they are the only ones around. If you almost run them over with your car, you will get the middle finger and an angry face, or an insulting outcry. They ride on the sidewalk, and you are expected to get out of the way. It is strange but true: cyclists are the "kings of the road." You can choose to be annoyed or simply accept this as a fact of life in the Netherlands.

All over the world, people associate the Netherlands with tulips, windmills, and wooden shoes. Tourism thrives on it. In real life, however, tulips (*tulpen*) only bloom in early spring, but most windmills (*molens*) are still operational, with the rest serving as decoration. As for wooden shoes (*klompen*)... you will have a hard time finding a store that sells them. They are considered a thing of the past, but you might occasionally find them on farms. There are still some wooden shoemakers (*klompenmakers*), but it is largely a retired craft. Whenever there is a folkloric event, though, the old-fashioned costumes and wooden shoes are part of the outfit.

Vocabulary - Dutch Special Days and Events

de bakfiets - cargo bike

de bloembol - flower bulb

de Bevrijdingsdag, 5 mei - Liberation Day, May 5, (WWII)

het bollenveld - bulb field

dit is nogal persoonlijk voor me - This is pretty personal for me

ik wil daar niet op antwoorden - I don't want to answer that

de fiets - bicycle

het fietspad - bicycle road

ik praat daar liever niet over - I'd rather not talk about that

de kerstman - Santa Claus

de klomp - wooden shoe

de klompenmaker - wooden shoemakers

de Koningsdag, 27 april - King's Day, April 27

de Koning - king

de Koningin - queen

de molen - windmill

de prins – prince

de prinses – princess

Sinterklaas – Saint Nicolas

De vrijmarkt – garage sale

zeg het gewoon – just say so

Zwarte Piet – Black Pete

Now you will continue with some helpful conversations, terms, and phrases related to traveling around the Netherlands.

Traveling and Sightseeing

By air

You: Goedemorgen, hier is mijn paspoort – Good morning, here's my passport

Steward: Dank u wel – Thank you

Stew: Hebt u ruimbagage? – Do you have hold luggage?

Stew: Wil u ook bagage inchecken? – Do you have check-in luggage?

You: Ja, een koffer – Yes, one suitcase

You: Nee, alleen handbagage – No, just carry-on

Stew: Uw koffer is te zwaar – Your suitcase is too heavy

Stew: U moet bijbetalen of er iets uithalen – You have to take some things out or pay extra

You: O jee, daar heb ik niet op gerekend – Oh my, I didn't count on that

You: Ik betaal wel bij. Ik heb alles nodig – I will pay extra; I need everything in it

Stew: Oké, dat kunt u bij balie xx doen – Okay, you can settle the balance at counter xxx

You: Ik moet overstappen – I have a transfer

Stew: Ik heb uw baggage doorgelabeld – I have labeled your luggage to its final destination

Stew: Maakt u zich geen zorgen – Don't you worry

Stew: De gate gaat zo dicht. U moet echt opschieten nu – The gate is closing any minute now. You must really hurry now

You: Oké, ik ben al weg! – Okay, I am on my way!

Stew: ik heb geen drie stoelen naast elkaar – I don't have three seats next to each other

You: Hè, wat jammer! Nou, dan maar apart – Darn! Too bad. Well, separate seats it is...

You: Zitten we wel bij elkaar in de buurt? – Are our seats close to one another?

Stew: Ja, dat gaat wel lukken – Yes, we can arrange that

Stew: U moet uiterlijk om x uur bij de gate zijn – You must be at the gate at xxx o'clock at the latest

Stew: De vlucht wordt niet omgeroepen – There won't be an announcement for your flight

You: Oké, dank u wel – Okay, thank you

You: Goededag, mijn bagage is niet aangekomen – Good day, my luggage didn't arrive

You: Ik heb die spullen echt nu nodig – I need my things now

Other: U kunt bij het eind van de bagagebanden een formulier invullen – You can file a form over there, at the end of the luggage belts

Other: U krijgt uw koffer dan morgen op uw adres afgeleverd – You will get your luggage delivered at your address tomorrow

You: maar ik heb nú spullen uit mijn koffer nodig! – But I need things from my suitcase now!

Other: Het spijt me heel erg... – I am very sorry...

Other: Gaat u alstublieft naar het kantoor bij het einde van de banden – Please, go to the luggage office at the end of the belts

You: Daar wordt u verder geholpen – They will further assist you

Other: Uw handbagage moet in het ruim – Your carry-on luggage must be checked in

You: Maar dat is mijn handbagage! – But that is my hand luggage!

Other: Het spijt me, alle bagagevakken in de cabine zijn vol – I am so sorry, there is no more room in the overhead bin

You: Mijn hemel... dan moet ik wel een een paar dingen eruit halen die ik aan boord nodig heb – Oh my, I must take out some things I need on board

Other: Gaat uw gang, daarna check ik uw handbagage in – Go ahead, I will then check-in your bag

You: Ik vind dit heel vervelend... – This is really annoying...

Other: Het spijt me, maar er is niets aan te doen – I am sorry, there is nothing I can do

Vocabulary – By Plane

aankomen – to arrive

aankomen (gewicht) – to gain weight

de aankomst – arrival

afleveren – to deliver

apart (van stoelen) – separate (seat)

apart (vreemd) – unique, special, peculiar

de bagage – luggage

de bagageband – luggage belt

het bagagevak – overhead bin

de balie – counter

bijbetalen – to pay extra

daarna – afterward

eruit halen – to take out

het formulier – form

de handbagage – carry-on

invullen – to fill in

de koffer – suitcase

lukken – to manage

maak je geen zorgen – don't worry

naast elkaar – next to each other

nodig hebben – to need

omroepen – to announce

overstappen – to transfer

het paspoort – passport

rekenen op – to count on

de ruimbagage – check-in luggage

de stoel – seat

het vertrek – departure

vervelend – annoying

vlak bij elkaar – close to each other

de vlucht (vliegtuig) – flight

de vlucht (ontsnappen) – to run, to escape, to flight

te zwaar – too heavy

zwaar – heavy

By Bus

You: Is dit de bus naar Rotterdam? – Is this the bus to Rotterdam?

Other: Nee, deze gaat naar Delft. Die voor Rotterdam is daar, op perron E - No, this one goes to Delft. The one tonRotterdam is over there, platform E

You: Dank u wel - Thank you

You: Gaat u naar Rotterdam? - Are you going to Rotterdam?

Other: Ja, over vier minuten vertrek ik - Yes, I will leave in four minutes

You: Fijn! Ben ik net op tijd! - Oh good! I am right on time then!

You: Stopt u ook bij het station? - Do you stop at the station?

Other: Jazeker, dat is mijn eindpunt - Sure do, that is the end of the route

You: Toppie! Twee keer graag - Great! Two persons, please

Other: Hebt u een ov-chipkaart? - Do you have an OV-chipcard?

You: Nee, die heb ik niet - No, I don't

Other: Hmm... dan koopt u twee losse ritten. Dat is wel een stuk duurder - Hmm... then you have to buy two separate rides. That is far more expensive

You: Jammer dan, ik moet nu meerijden - Too bad, but I need this ride

Other: Prima, dat is dan € xxx - Fine, that will be € xxx

Other: Blijft u hier lang? - Will you be staying here long?

You: Nou, wel een paar weken, ja - Well, a couple of weeks for sure

Other: Dan kunt u beter twee chipkaarten kopen die u kunt opladen. Dat is een stuk voordeliger voor u - Then you'd better buy two chipcards you can top up. That is way better for your wallet

You: Dank u wel voor de tip! - Thank you for the tip!

Vocabulary - By Bus

de bus - bus

duur - expensive

jammer dan - too bad

los - separate

net op tijd - right on time

het Openbaar Vervoer (ov) - public transport

opladen - to top up

de ov-chipcard - OV-chipcard

een paar weken - a couple of weeks

het perron - platform

de rit - ride

een stuk duurder - far more expensive

het stuk - piece/play/part

een stuk beter - way better

top(pie)!(popular use only) - great!

By Train

You: Waar vertrekt de trein naar Arnhem? - From where does the train to Arnhem leave?

Other: Van perron 5b. Als u vlug bent, haalt u hem nog net - From platform 5b. If you are quick you can catch it right now

Other: Anders moet u een half uur wachten op de volgende trein - If you miss it, you will have to wait half an hour for the next one

You: Moet ik overstappen? - Do I need to change/transfer trains?

Other: Nee, dit is een directe trein - No, this is a direct train

You: Ik sta al heel lang te wachten – I am waiting for quite some time now

Other: Het spijt me, de trein heeft vertraging. Het duurt nog twintig minuten – I am sorry, there is a delay. It will take another twenty minutes.

You: Maar er is helemaal niets omgeroepen – But there has been no announcement at all

Other: Oh nee? Oei, dat is niet zo netjes – No? Oh, that is not right

Other: Dat moet een vergissing zijn – That must be a mistake

Other: We geven altijd een update over vertragingen – We always give an update regarding delays

Vocabulary – By Train

altijd – always

direct – direct

duren – to take

geven – to give

halen (de trein/bus/vliegtuig) – to catch (train/bus/plane)

niet zo netjes – not right

omroepen – to make an announcement

omroepen (tv/radio) – to broadcast (TV/radio)

overstappen – to change/transfer

het perron – platform

staan te wachten – to be waiting

de vergissing – mistake

de vertraging – delay

vertrekken – to leave

vlug – quick

wachten – to wait

de update – update

Sightseeing

You: Hallo, kunt u mij wat informatie geven over leuke dingen om te zien? – Hello, can you give me some information about sightseeing here?

You: Of dingen om te bezoeken of te doen? – Or things to visit or to do?

Other: Daar staat een heel rek met informatie – Over there you will find a rack full of information

Other: Ik kan iets voor u reserveren – I can make a reservation for you

Other: We hebben ook entreekaartjes – We have entry tickets as well

Other: Dat scheelt tijd, u hoeft dan niet in de rij te staan – That will save you some time, you don't have to stand in line

Other: We hebben hier een gidsje met informatie – We have a booklet with information

Other: Voor meer informatie kunt u naar de VVV gaan – For more information you'd better go to the tourism information office (VVV)

Other: Hun kantoor is vlakbij. Twee straten verderop – Their office is nearby. Two streets away

You: Dank u wel! – Thank you!

Other: Geen dank – You're welcome

You: Hallo, kunt u me zeggen hoe ik naar het Van Gogh museum moet lopen? – Hello, can you tell me the way to the Van Gogh museum, please?

You: Ik snap niets van die plattegrond op mijn smartphone... – I don't get this map on my smartphone...

Other: O jee! Het is niet ver meer, hoor - Oh my! It's not far anymore

Other: Volg gewoon deze straat en ga dan rechtsaf bij het verkeerslicht - Just continue on this street and take a right at the traffic light

Other: Na zo'n 200 meter gaat u dan linksaf - After about 200 meters you take a left

Other: En dan ligt het min of meer recht voor u - And then it is right in front of you, more or less

You: Dank u wel! - Thank you so much!

Other: Geen dank. Veel plezier! - You're welcome. Have fun!

You: ik heb kaarten online gekocht - I bought tickets online

You: Moet ik dan nog steeds in de rij gaan staan om binnen te komen? - Do I still have to stand in line to get in?

Other: Nee hoor, juist niet. U kunt via die poort naar binnen - No, no, not at all. You can enter through that gate

Other: Daar scannen ze uw entreebewijzen - They will scan your admission tickets right there

You: Hoe laat mag de volgende groep naar binnen? - What time can the next group enter?

Other: Elke twintig minuten mogen er maximaal 40 mensen naar binnen - Every twenty minutes a maximum of 40 people can/may enter

You: O jee, en er zijn zoveel mensen! - Oh my, there are so many people!

Other: Daarom reguleren we de stroom bezoekers - That's why we regulate the flow of visitors

Other: Anders heeft u weinig plezier van uw bezoek hier - If not, you won't enjoy your visit much here

Other: En dat is niet de bedoeling – And that's not what we want

You: Nou, vooruit dan maar. Ik had niet gedacht dat het zo druk zou zijn... – Oh well, all right. I didn't think it would be that crowded...

Other: Alleen 's winters is het rustiger – Only in winter it is quieter

Vocabulary – Sightseeing

Alleen – only

de bedoeling – intention/purpose

bezoeken – to visit

de bezoeker – visitor

binnenkomen/-gaan – to get in/to enter

het entreekaartje – entry ticket

het entreebewijs – admission ticket

de informatie – information

doen – to do

druk (= veel mensen) – crowded

druk (= machines) – pression/pressure

druk (= veel werk) – busy

druk (= karakter) – zappy/lively/active

de druk (= boek etc) – print

de gids – brochure/guide

het gidsje – booklet

in de herfst – in autumn

het kantoor – office

in de lente – in spring

leuke dingen om te zien – sightseeing

linksaf gaan – to take a left

oh jee! – oh my!

ongeveer – about

meer (= niet meer) – anymore

min of meer – more or less/so to speak

niet ver – not far

plezier hebben – to have fun

de poort – gate

recht voor u(w neus) – right in front of you

rechtsaf gaan – to take a right

het rek – rack

reguleren – to regulate

reserveren – to make a reservation/to book

de rij – line

rustig – quiet

de straat – street

de stroom – flow

de stroom – electricity

tijd schelen – to save time

scannen – to scan

veel plezier – have fun

ver – far

verderop – away

vlakbij – nearby

volgen – to follow

de VVV – tourist information office

weg – away

's winters – in winter

's zomers – in summer

Some Sayings and Proverbs

Like any language, Dutch has a lot of proverbs and sayings. Some are centuries old, half a century old, or still in use and considered "old-fashioned." Language is alive and continuously changing.

Now it is time to conclude your basic learning of Dutch with a few common sayings and proverbs.

As mentioned, not everybody will understand your Dutch right away. If your pronunciation is not the way it should be, some Dutch people might not understand you. However, don't worry about it too much, you will get there. Besides, your Dutch might be way better than their French, Russian, Chinese, Greek, Bahasa, or whatever your native language is!

A few sayings:

Een foto zegt meer dan 1,000 woorden – A picture is worth 1,000 words

Het ijs breken – To break the ice

Appels met peren vergelijken – Comparing apples to oranges

Achter de wolken schijnt de zon – Every cloud has a silver lining

Wat niet weet, dat niet deert – Ignorance is bliss

Je kunt niet alles hebben – You can't have your cake and eat it too

De stilte voor de storm – The calm before the storm

Zo gezond als een vis – Fit as a fiddle

Door dik en dun – In good times and in bad times

Tijd is geld – Time is money

Beter laat dan nooit – Better late than never

Een goed begin is het halve werk – Well begun is half done

Als je over de duivel praat! – Speak of the devil!

And proverbs:

Iets met een korreltje zout nemen – Take it with a grain of salt

Beter één vogel in de hand dan tien in de lucht – A bird in the hand is worth two in the bush

De huid niet verkopen voordat de beer geschoten is – Don't count your chickens before they hatch

Twee vliegen in één klap – Kill two birds with one stone

Een storm in een glas water – A storm in a teacup

Haastige spoed is zelden goed – Haste makes waste

Geen slapende honden wakker maken – Let sleeping dogs lie

De pot verwijt de ketel dat hij zwart ziet – The pot calling the kettle black

Van de wal in de sloot – Out of the frying pan and into the fire

Tiny Tasks Answers

#1:

13 = dertien; 8 = acht; 27 = zevenentwintig; 63 = drieënzestig; 78 = achtenzeventig; 104 = honderdvier; 12 = twaalf; 140 = honderdveertig; 549 = vijfhonderdnegenenveertig; 636 = zeshonderdzesendertig; 244 = tweehonderdvierenveertig; 82 = tweeëntachtig

#5:

Conjugation of some verbs:

Bedoelen = ik bedoel, jij/u bedoelt, hij/zij/het bedoelt, wij/jullie/zij bedoelen

Bouwen = ik bouw, jij/u bouwt, hij/zij/het bouwt, wij/jullie/zij bouwen

Branden = ik brand, jij/u brandt, hij/zij/het brandt, wij/jullie/zij branden

Drinken = ik drink, jij/u drinkt, hij/zij/het drinkt, wij/jullie/zij drinken

Huilen = ik huil, jij/u huilt, hij/zij/u huilt, wij/jullie/zij huilen

Kijken = ik kijken, jij/u kijkt, hij/zij/het kijkt, wij/jullie/zij kijken

Lachen – ik lach, jij/u lacht, hij/zij/het lacht, wij/jullie/zij lachen

Rijden = ik rijd, jij/u rijdt, hij/zij/het rijdt, wij/jullie/zij rijden

Vloeien = ik vloei, jij/u vloeit, hij/zij/het vloeit, wij/jullie/zij vloeien

Voeren = ik voer, jij/u voert, hij/zij/het voert, wij/jullie/zij voeren

Wandelen = ik wandel, jij//u wandelt, hij/zij/het wandelt, wij/jullie/zij wandelen

#6:

Making sentences:

Hij eet een lekkere maaltijd

Wij planten allerlei bloemen

Jij leest een goede krant

Ik was de vuile kleren

Zij drinkt warme thee

Jullie strijken het blauwe overhemd

Ik schrijf een lange brief

Jij geeft een klein cadeau

Zij hebben een grote hond

Ik koop nieuwe schoenen

#8:

Past tense (ovt) of the following verbs:

koken – kookte

wonen – woonde

fietsen – fietste

rollen – rolde

draaien – draaide

fotograferen – fotografeerde

graaien – graaide

lachen – lachte

sjouwen – sjouwde

Conclusion

Congratulations on making it through to the end of this book! Hopefully, you found it both insightful and fun!

Learning a language is just like learning to drive. You start with the basics, then practice, practice, and practice some more. And soon enough, you have mastered the art!

Now, you can engage in Dutch conversations and experiences, and put all your newly acquired knowledge to the test.

Veel succes! Good luck!

Acknowledgements

This book could not have been written without the following websites:

https://onzetaal.nl/taaladvies

www.ikschrijfbeter.nl

www.uilentaal.wordpress.com

www.leerboek.nl

www.mijnwoordenboek.nl

www.ef.nl

CPSIA information can be obtained
at www.ICGtesting.com
Printed in the USA
LVHW081537271020
669962LV00009B/210